The Professional Woman's Guide to Conflict Management

Indispensable tools, tips, and techniques for your workplace

Elinor Robin, PhD

Impackt Publishing
We Mean Business

The Professional Woman's Guide to Conflict Management

First published: October 2014

Production reference: 1161014

Published by Impackt Publishing Ltd.
Livery Place
35 Livery Street
Birmingham B3 2PB, UK.

ISBN 978-1-78300-024-1

www.Impacktpub.com

Credits

Author
Elinor Robin, PhD

Reviewer
Susan F. Dubow

Acquisition Editor
Nick Falkowski

Content Development Editor
Vaibhav Pawar

Copy Editors
Tanvi Bhatt

Karuna Narayanan

Project Coordinator
Venitha Cutinho

Proofreaders
Simran Bhogal

Paul Hindle

Production Coordinator
Melwyn D'sa

Cover Work
Simon Cardew

About the Author

Elinor Robin, PhD, is a mediator and mediation trainer whose mission is to help men and women discover better ways to look at, respond to, and overcome their professional and personal conflicts. With wit, wisdom, and passion, Elinor brings her clients and students the benefit of her revolutionary spirit, vision, small business expertise, and extensive court system experience. She has mediated thousands of disputes and has developed a powerful method for analyzing and resolving the conflicts that we face within our families, workplaces, and communities. As a mediation trainer, Elinor goes beyond information sharing, engaging her audiences with candor and compassion. Her innovative training programs have prepared over 12,000 professional mediators to handle the conflicts they regularly face. To learn more about Elinor and how her 25 years of research and practical experience can help you, visit http://www.ElinorRobin.com.

Acknowledgments

This book has been a long time in coming. It is a reflection of much of my learning, teaching, and work over the last 25 years. I could not possibly thank all of the people who contributed to this project because almost everyone who has crossed my path has had a hand in teaching me what I needed to know to make this book a reality. Certainly, special acknowledgement is owed to my immediate and extended family members. As I see it, this book was developed on the foundation of support you show me. And, it will be a part of the legacy I will always share with you.

The Professional Woman's Guide to Conflict Management is not my first attempt to get my words in print. Throughout my earlier writing attempts, I have had countless supporters. So many of my friends, students, clients, and a variety of professional helpers have made a contribution to my writing endeavors. Special thanks are in order to Kate Shockey, HR Manager with the Volusia County Clerk of Courts, for her review of an earlier version of my work, and Kellie Keucha, who convinced me how important it is that I keep writing. As to this book, I want to thank professional women, Heather Trapani Bassett, Elizabeth Dilts, and Evelyn Ziegler for their willingness to share their wisdom with me.

Ultimately, this book would not have happened without the team at Impackt Publishing. I don't know how Pritesh D'souza found me, but I am so glad he did. Nick Falkowski and the staff—Tanvi Bhatt, Simon Cardew, Venitha Cutinho, Richard Gall, Rebecca Lawley, Vaibhav Pawar, Faisal Siddiqui, and Danielle Rosen—made this book a reality. My fellow Impackt author, Lauren M. Hug, generously provided mentorship and vision throughout the writing process and has become a trusted friend and colleague. Thank you all for the amazing gift we are launching here together.

About the Reviewer

Susan F. Dubow, a pioneer in the field of Alternative Dispute Resolution (ADR), has had a long and distinguished career. She served as the Director of the Court Mediation and Arbitration Program, the ADR Division of the 17th Judicial Circuit, Broward County, Florida, for over 22 years. In 2000, she co-founded Mediation Training Group. Today, Mediation Training Group is a leading provider of mediation training, and Susan serves as its President and CEO. Susan mediates workplace disputes for both the Equal Employment Opportunity Commission and the US Postal Service; she is an Adjunct Professor at Nova Southeastern University's Shepard Broad Law Center; Vice-chair of the Florida Supreme Court's Mediation Ethics Advisory Board (MEAC); and a past-president of both The Association of South Florida Mediators and Arbitrators (ASFMA) and The Florida Academy of Professional Mediators (FAPM).

*"One can live magnificently in this world, if one knows how to work
and how to love….."*

–Leo Tolstoy

*This book is dedicated to my partners in work and in love. Thank you Susan and David for my
magnificent life.*

Contents

Chapter 7: Making Conflict Management Happen in Your Workplace

Preface

In the perfect workplace, everyone gets along. There are no disputes regarding titles, compensation, schedules, assignments, or environmental conditions. There are no personality conflicts and there is no sexual harassment. Each worker takes full responsibility for his or her actions and never attempts to place blame on another person or an external influence. Do you recognize this place? No? You are not alone.

For most professional women, the "perfect" workplace doesn't exist. Instead, many of us find ourselves working harder and longer with fewer resources. Isolated from the support of the traditional extended family, we routinely juggle home and work responsibilities. No wonder our offices and organizations often feel like conflict breeding grounds.

As a little girl, you were likely told to play nice, share, be polite, and avoid unpleasantness. Actually, even if no one said these things directly, this is the message that most Western cultures transmit to their female children. Additionally, scientists have recently determined that there is an evolutionary "tend and befriend" survival behavior that females (human and some other animals) have adopted in addition to the physiological "fight-or-flight" response we share with men. In light of this "tend and befriend" programming, it's no surprise that many women see conflict as such a negative struggle.

Looking ahead, as women continue to expand their influence and participation in the workplace, it seems clear that issues such as sexual harassment, discrimination, health hazards, the negative stereotyping of a parent's role in the workplace, and the competing demands of job and family will continue to cause workplace conflicts. Additionally, unresolved and mismanaged conflicts driven by bruised egos, uncontrolled emotions, and mean-spirited behaviors have the potential to negatively impact your bottom line and your professional reputation.

Conflict can indeed be destructive when individual agendas are fulfilled by discrediting the other party (who is now designated as "the enemy"). There is, however, some good news: it is possible to avoid the destructive consequences of workplace conflict! You can, in fact, decode and de-escalate the conflicts that are simmering and erupting in your workplace. This book was written to give you a how-to road map.

Ultimately, the knowledge you gain from reading this book will lead to an increased sense of comfort and conscious conflict ownership regarding your workplace disputes. (I define conscious conflict ownership as the ability to look at your conflicts and clearly see how you created or co-created the situation, where you are, and where you could be.) Ultimately, as you increase your conscious conflict ownership, you will be able to convey a stronger sense of commitment to the people, projects, and organizations you are connected to. Amazingly, when we are able to embrace and work through everyday conflicts, the end result is usually enhanced productivity and connections. These are conflict's true gifts.

Instead of using the terms "dispute resolution" or "conflict resolution," the term "conflict management" is used here intentionally. Many conflicts, especially those where the parties involved have an on-going relationship, cannot be solved or re-solved on a permanent basis. At best, these conflicts can be managed. In this instance, "managed" doesn't mean to control or govern, it means "to care for," like you manage your investments, or "to handle," as in, "he managed while his wife was out of town."

The role that women play in the workplace is continuing to evolve. Likewise, the strategies that we use to manage our workplace conflicts will need on-going evaluation. After spending the last 25 years studying conflict and relationships, I am still often amazed by the complexities in our interactions. I am delighted to be able to share my knowledge and philosophy with you.

What this book covers

Chapter 1, All About Conflict, explains conflict dynamics, including what conflict is, how conflict unfolds in our interpersonal relationships, the physiological factors that drive our conflicts, and how you can calm your body and save yourself from conflict drama.

Chapter 2, Women at Work, discusses the impact gender has on us and our work, and outlines the components of successful business partnerships and workplace friendships.

Chapter 3, Workplace Conflict in the New Normal – The Reasons and the Costs, uncovers the hidden causes and costs of modern-day workplace conflict. Advanced strategies for dealing with conflict, power imbalances, and value misalignments are also presented.

Chapter 4, Conflict Management Styles, Strategies, and Methods, considers and evaluates specific negation styles and conflict management methods so that you can learn to use them to your advantage.

Chapter 5, Becoming an Expert Conflict Manager – Self-reflection and Skill Development, focuses on skill development and how you can use conscious conflict ownership, negotiation, and listening to diffuse the conflicts you encounter.

Chapter 6, Conflict Conversations, prepares you to use conversation to clear the air and create a sense of connection by providing you with a format for holding a difficult discussion, techniques for analyzing a conflict, guidelines for fighting smart and fighting fair, and tips for making magical apologies.

Chapter 7, Making Conflict Management Happen in Your Workplace, offers techniques that foster employee loyalty and instructions for designing a conflict management system for your workplace.

Who this book is for

If you're a professional woman and want to learn how to confidently and successfully manage conflict, then this book will give you the tools you need.

Conventions

In this book, you will find a number of styles of text that distinguish between different kinds of information. Here are some examples of these styles, and an explanation of their meaning.

New terms and **important words** are shown in bold.

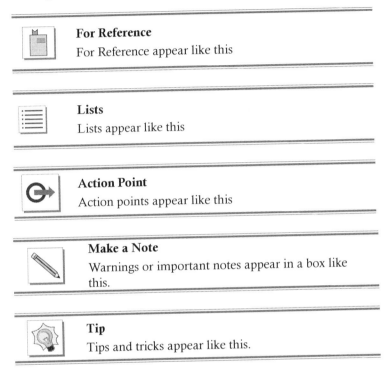

For Reference

For Reference appear like this

Lists

Lists appear like this

Action Point

Action points appear like this

Make a Note

Warnings or important notes appear in a box like this.

Tip

Tips and tricks appear like this.

Reader feedback

Feedback from our readers is always welcome. Let us know what you think about this book—what you liked or may have disliked. Reader feedback is important for us to develop titles that you really get the most out of.

To send us general feedback, simply send an e-mail to feedback@impacktpub.com, and mention the book title via the subject of your message.

Piracy

Piracy of copyrighted material on the Internet is an ongoing problem across all media. At Packt, we take the protection of our copyright and licenses very seriously. If you come across any illegal copies of our works, in any form, on the Internet, please provide us with the location address or website name immediately so that we can pursue a remedy.

Please contact us at `copyright@impacktpub.com` with a link to the suspected pirated material.

We appreciate your help in protecting our authors, and our ability to bring you valuable content.

>1

All About Conflict

Each of us views every aspect of life from a unique perspective. Your perspective is shaped by the distinct combination of your experiences, cultural makeup, personality factors, and needs. Our conflicts are the inevitable and natural reflections of these constantly evolving differences.

Pause for just a moment and search your memory bank. Can you remember a time when a conflict at work resulted in greater understanding? When conflicts are managed well, they can provide a forum for a healthy voicing of concerns. Have you experienced a time when dialogue brought you or your co-workers towards a clarification of roles, a pathway to draw upon collective wisdom, a means to discover new options, or a plan for a better way to do things?

Hopefully, you have had one of these experiences. Sadly, however, you may be much more familiar with mismanaged conflicts. When conflicts are mismanaged, they can erupt into violence or slowly snowball, as egos and emotions aggrivate the original irritant beyond recognition. This book was written so you can have more positive conflict experiences and fewer negative ones.

Conflicts play out in our lives in two distinct ways. Sometimes, we are involved as a party in a dispute. Other times, we are drawn into a conflict as a third person who plays the role of advisor, comforter, or mediator to one or both of the people involved. Ultimately, at some point in your professional career, it is likely that you will find yourself in both of these roles. The latter is especially applicable if you supervise others and are aware of your staff members' quarrels.

This chapter will provide you with the knowledge you need to manage the conflicts you face as a party in conflict. You will also learn what you need to know about conflicts so that you can better manage the disputes that you encounter as an outsider or third person looking in.

Managing conflict is a cyclical process that requires constant practice. The more experience you gain in addressing conflict, the more adept you will become at untangling and decoding the conflicts you face. At the end of this section, you will view conflict through a different lens. You will understand the following:

➤ How inconsistent or divergent expectations cause conflict

➤ How the **fight-or-flight survival response** influences our conflict behaviors

➤ How to calm lower brain reactions and move towards reason and reasonableness

➤ How we perform the roles of victim, hero, and villain in our conflicts

➤ How to avoid escalating the conflicts you face

What is conflict?

What is conflict? There is no clear consensus among the experts. We all know conflict when we see it, but it's not easy to define. Sometimes we hear talk of conflict being about limited resources. However, people who know how to work together can usually find ways to distribute their resources without engaging in destructive conflict. Fundamentalists (of any kind) would have us believe that conflict is the result (or symptom) of insurmountable differences in values and beliefs. This idea is misleading. In most cases, people can overcome significant differences when they are willing to engage in a mature dialogue.

Make a note

Conflict is best defined as "the by-product of inconsistent or incompatible perceptions and expectations regarding what is, what could be, or what should be."

Frequently, even the hint of inconsistent or incompatible expectations unconsciously translates to mean that the person on the other side is somehow being dismissive or disrespectful. Like a tinderbox, the sense of being dismissed, discounted, disrespected, or devalued, which is present in almost every human conflict, leaves us vulnerable to an emotional explosion. Knowing this will help you find and define the "dis" that points to a conflict's true germ or starting point, even when the people involved cover it up with anger or monetary claims.

Case study

Marvin told me this story of a conflict during a workplace training session:

"Our office recently experienced a significant coffee conflict. We have a coffee club. Staffers who want to participate and drink the coffee are asked to make a monthly $5 donation to cover the cost of supplies. When it became common knowledge that one of the workers, Dorothy, was drinking coffee but not contributing, another staff member, Kelly, turned on the elderly Dorothy like a rabid dog. Kelly's anger did not fit Dorothy's crime. As the supervisor, I offered to make the contribution for Dorothy so that everyone could put this behind them and get back to work. That only made things worse. The office became divided, polarized along generational lines. Ultimately, Kelly was able to move beyond the $5 distraction and present me with a long list of incidents where Dorothy's behavior had upset her. While each occurrence on the list had left Kelly feeling dismissed, discounted, or disrespected, she had said nothing until the coffee skirmish. This was the first time that Kelly could place an actual dollar amount on Dorothy's grumpy demeanor. The $5 became the symbol for all of the times Dorothy had behaved in a way that Kelly interpreted as Dorothy positioning herself above having to follow the rules."

Ultimately, when Dorothy's position was revealed, it became apparent that she had consistently interpreted her younger coworkers' attitudes as devaluing of her skill set and institutional memory. In this case, as in most cases of workplace conflict, there were two sides to the story. Until we know the rest of the story, we don't really have the full picture. When you are a third party—like Marvin in this case—avoid jumping to conclusions based on one person's side of the story.

Expectations are typically the outcome of one-sided secret deals we cook up in our own heads and hearts. These unspoken expectations almost always create disappointments. Kelly had expectations for how she wanted Dorothy to behave towards her. Dorothy did not share these expectations. She saw Kelly as a sassy know-it-all and responded to her accordingly. You may have already learned that "expectation is the root of all heartache. "(This quote is sometimes attributed to Shakespeare; the exact origin is actually unknown.) So, a key strategy for productive conflict management is moving expectations out of the shadows. When we are able to clarify the differences between our realities and our expectations, we can deal with disappointments before they sprout off into destructive conflict.

Each time we engage in conflict, three separate forces come into play. They are as follows:

> ➤ First, specific physiological changes happen within our brains and our bodies
> ➤ Next, each person in conflict takes actions (employs behaviors) to defend him or herself from some perceived threat
> ➤ Finally, the reactions and responses of the two people involved create the interactive dance of conflict that they engage in together

In the next three sections, we will look at each of these forces more closely.

Conflict physiology and the brain

If you expect one thing, and your coworker expects something else, chances are each of you will come to assume that your individual needs are not going to be met. When this happens, instinctively, you are each pushed into a **fight-or-flight survival response**. The part of your brain called **the reptilian brain** becomes activated. As you kick into high emotional gear, another part of the brain, your limbic system starts producing adrenaline and other powerful hormones. The reptilian brain and the limbic system are stronger and more automatic than your cerebral cortex, the thinking (or reasoning) part of the human brain. As the limbic system rushes hormones through your body, you intuitively move into defense mode. A desire for blood, vengeance, or validation may be evoked. Alternatively, you may want to rush and hide under the bed. Either way, physical symptoms such as a rapid increase in heart rate and blood pressure, excessive or shallow breathing, sweating, and trembling may become evident.

Make a note

Until you can bring your physiology under control, your ability to negotiate, reason, and empathize is reduced.

This physiological fight-or-flight response may have served our prehistoric ancestors as they ran from wild animals or fought with neighboring tribes. However, it does not serve you well in the modern workplace. Without a sense of safety, it is likely you will react to perceived threats in this primordial way; it's programmed into your biochemistry. STOP!! This can be detrimental to your career.

Make a note

Don't do anything while your reptile brain is in charge!

How to calm your reptile brain

It is possible to calm your reptile brain and limbic system and move back into your cerebral cortex where you can reason and be reasonable. Mediator Stephen Kotev believes that we can train our bodies to more effectively manage the symptoms of the fight-or-flight response. He teaches body-awareness skills that are derived from the Japanese martial art of Aikido. For most of us, learning Aikido is not an option. However, there are some body-awareness techniques you can utilize when a perceived threat moves you out of your thinking brain. These include deep or focused breathing, reading your body, meditation or prayer, and journaling.

Deep or focused breathing

One of my favorite breathing techniques is **heart-breathing**. This method of focused breathing can help you relieve physiological symptoms in a matter of seconds.

Action Point

Focus your attention on the area around your heart and breathe into that space. Then, breathe out from your heart. As you slowly breathe into and through your heart, in your mind's eye, visualize something or someone that you are very grateful for. Hold this image as you take some additional breaths.

You will be amazed at the difference this can make in a very short time.

Reading your body

Action Point

Quietly sit or stand. Feel your feet firmly connecting to the ground beneath you. Beginning with this sense of grounded feet, slowly scan your body from the inside out. What sensations do you feel as you make a toe-to-head assessment? What hurts? Where is there tension? Try moving and stretching to loosen up the parts that are holding tension. If you are feeling strong emotions, it's often wise to simply sit and let the emotional energy pass through you.

Meditation or prayer

It has been said that prayer is talking to God, and meditation is listening to God. Many people find one or both of these activities comforting.

Action Point

Even if you are not drawn to either prayer or meditation, you may still find it soothing to repeat a positive affirmation to yourself over and over again. My favorites are *"I love and approve of myself"* and *"I am safe and all is well in my world."*

Journaling

Stream-of-consciousness writing is unstructured, unedited writing that explores your perceptions or feelings about a certain person, event, or situation.

Action Point

Just grab a pen and paper and start writing. Let it all out. Hopefully, when you are done, you will experience a sense of clarity or cleansing relief. Most of the time, it is best to keep this writing private. If you decide to share with a trusted confidant, make sure they understand and are in agreement regarding the level of confidentiality that you expect.

These techniques will not work unless you practice them. The time to practice is not when you are in the throes of a fight-or-flight reactive response. Instead, experiment and find the calming activity that works best for you when there is no perceived threat. Frequent practicing will make moving into your activity easier when your reptile brain and limbic system get fired up and start pushing you into survival (also known as lunatic) mode.

The victim, hero, villain dance

A workplace conflict can become a strange variation of musical chairs. Instead of changing chairs, the two players move between three roles: an evil doer, a beautiful victim princess, and a noble rescuer prince.

The victim

In this fairy tale triangle of villain, victim, and hero, the victim is under attack, powerless and inclined to withdraw. When we play the victim, we absolve ourselves of responsibility. After all, as an innocent person, the conflict is not our fault. Rather than meeting the situation head-on, we justify inaction by telling ourselves that the other person is the villain and needs to change or be stopped.

The hero

Sometimes, we shift into the hero mode to protect ourselves, defend our interests, and even the score. It's a role full of courage, selflessness, and the dramatic seeking of justice. Of course, the darker side is that as heroes, we can become self-righteous, manipulative, and controlling. Bringing in the hero usually heightens the conflict.

The villain

While we have no difficulty pointing to the villain when we find ourselves in conflict, ironically, the villain usually views himself as the victim in the conflict, and like us, conjures up his own hero to fight back.

This concept may be easier to understand if you think in terms of good and evil. When I am in conflict, I see myself as good and my adversary as evil. On the other side, my adversary sees themselves as good and me as evil. Each one of us strikes out in order to protect ourselves and annihilate the evil perpetrator on the other side. In truth, none of us are one sided. Simplistic, black-and-white worlds and characters fit in fairy tales but not in a complex real-life setting. In fact, the old adage, "it takes two to tango" holds very true when it comes to conflict.

The conflict action plan

Here are the conflict tips and truths you need to know to round out your conflict education.

Conflict truths

The closer we are, the more likely we will rub against one another

The more we rub, the more likely combustion will occur. Years ago, my husband, David, committed an atrocity, and I was furiously angry. (Right now, amazingly, I don't remember what he did, and for the sake of my sanity, I won't work too hard to recall the memory.) Anyway, after a long drawn-out discussion, I wanted him to promise that he would never do THAT (whatever it was) again. He said he would do his best, but while he was committed to making all efforts not to repeat this particular offense, he was sure that he would otherwise hurt or disappoint me again. He was right. How could it be otherwise? People who are close to one another, physically or emotionally, are much more likely to bump into and rub up against each other. Someone who is just a bit player in your life doesn't really have the ability to devastate you. However, those people who are closely connected to your career, which involves professional identity (the way you see yourself), professional reputation (the way others see you), and income, as well as the people you really care about in your personal life, do. So, even little slights, when they come from a primary player, can be excruciatingly painful.

Spot it, you got it

Frequently, psychological forces are operating beneath the surface of a given conflict. The process of projection may be used to explain the dynamics in some conflicts. Projection is a method of emotional self-preservation that allows us to place or project our own unacceptable, threatening, or repressed attributes, thoughts, motives, and emotions onto someone else. We then start to believe that these things are accurate. An example of projection is the woman who has secret fears of being incompetent. She buries and denies her fears and then concludes that her boss is incompetent.

What, how, and ouch – the three categories of conflicts

There are three different ways conflict plays out in our lives. The three categories of conflict are as follows:

> **Task conflicts**, which are debates over *what* we should do

> **Process conflicts**, which stem from the question of *how* we do the task at hand

> **Relationship** or **personality conflicts**, which tend to be power struggles fueled by emotional and ego-driven blowups

Task and process conflicts can be very productive as they are rooted in finding best practices. These are the conflicts that are opportunities to expand perspectives and investigate new options. Warning! Task and process conflicts, when ignored for too long, can be misinterpreted and inflamed. The end result is that they can become destructive relationship conflicts, full of suspicion and competition.

Relationship conflicts (the proverbial personality clash) revolve around personal attacks that seem to pop up on their own. Parties embroiled in relationship conflict will often engage in mean-spirited behaviors aimed at fulfilling individual agendas or discrediting the other party, who is designated as "the enemy." When faced with a relationship conflict, your first task is to stop the situation from escalating further.

We all need a mediator – sometimes

Early in this chapter I explained that conflicts play out in two ways. Sometimes we are the main characters in a conflict and sometimes we are drawn into someone else's conflict as a third party supporter. I wish I could honestly tell you that after reading this book, you will be able to manage all of your own conflicts, avoid dangerous emotional triggers, and never get your buttons pushed again. However, if I said that, I would be lying. On the other hand, I can tell you that a third person who is brave enough to intervene in someone else's conflict can bring about miraculous results. When a willing mediator is able to create a safe environment, emotional triggers can lose their charge. As the mediator gently pushes people in conflict away from emotional mayhem and into rational thinking, magic happens. Unfortunately, it is impossible to be both a mediator and a participant in a conflict. So, please share this book with a friend. We can—we must—act as each other's mediators.

Conflict tips

1. Avoid escalating the conflict

The following are some things that can escalate conflict and should be avoided:

- ➤ Losing your temper
- ➤ Overreacting
- ➤ Aggressive gestures
- ➤ Assuming that the problems will go away
- ➤ Waiting too long to step in
- ➤ Spending a lot of time trying to attach blame (faultfinding is looking backward; resolution requires moving forward)
- ➤ Treating warring parties like children
- ➤ Forcing apologies
- ➤ Dealing with private matters in public
- ➤ Using bully tactics
- ➤ Asking someone to compromise something that is really important, just to be a good sport (unwilling agreements often carry resentments that can cause more trouble later on)
- ➤ Expecting to find a flawless solution
- ➤ Reacting out of fear and anger

2. Be proactive, not reactive

Address conflict in a timely manner, before it becomes systemic. Denying that conflict exists or failing to respond to it promptly can be costly. Unresolved issues tend to fester and grow out of proportion. When a conflict cannot be immediately addressed, set a time and place for the meeting.

3. Listen to the whole story, without interrupting or making judgments

Often, people simply want someone to hear what they have to say.

When stories are inconsistent and/or the cause of the conflict is undeterminable, at the appropriate time, suggest wiping the slate clean and starting anew by putting the incident in the past.

4. Keep your cool

Uncontrolled emotions can harm your image, no matter how much you are provoked.

5. Say what you mean, but say it positively

Words and tone can convey powerful positive and negative images. Saying "How can I help you?" rather than "What do you want?" may be all it takes to stop a conflict from escalating. Realize that the way something is said is at least as important as what is said.

6. Encourage a team approach to problem solving

In some companies, a team approach may require a complete culture change.

7. Respect the other person's point of view

Even if you disagree with it, avoid belittling what someone else believes.

8. Be aware of cultural issues

Ask for explanations of cultural issues. It's okay to admit that you want or need clarification. Confront cultural discrimination in the workplace. Do not tolerate or go along with ethnic jokes or ridiculing.

9. Give feedback

A common problem with difficult behavior is that the person is unaware that their behavior is causing a problem. By giving timely feedback about specific behaviors, misunderstandings can sometimes be avoided and expectations clarified. A useful formula to give feedback that deals with both emotions and facts is using "**I-Statements**." For example:

> *"I feel frustrated when I am interrupted at our team meetings. It breaks my train of thought, and I struggle getting started again. I need time to finish with what I am saying. It would help me if we spoke one at a time and waited for each other to finish."*

Notice that this feedback formula is a four-part process that includes the following:

List

The "I feel" statement

The cause of my feeling

The impact on me

A request for resolution

Self-assessment

When you have time to sit and reflect, answer the following questions:

> How comfortable are you with the emotion-driven energy that lurks under most human conflicts?

> How comfortable are you with the venting that may have to happen before a conflict can be resolved?

Make a note

Think back, for just a moment, to the last time you found yourself embroiled in conflict. Can you still feel the physical sensations? Is the anger or rage still there, simmering? Much of the time, these feelings are just floating on the surface. Remember, you are safe. Allow the anger to move through you. Once it passes, are you able to identify a sense of feeling dismissed, discounted, disenfranchised, or disrespected? Keep in mind that the person on the other side may not have intended to trigger this sense of being devalued in you. If they did, it is likely it was in response to your triggering the same thing in them. Is there anything you need to do now in regard to this conflict?

Action steps

Consider a current unresolved conflict. Does it serve you well to work on getting this conflict resolved? What are your other options? Is it possible to reduce the level of contact or the number of interactions you have with the person on the other side? Is walking away or cutting off communications a viable option? What are the costs involved in ending this relationship? When you are clear, you can choose to follow these action points:

Action Point

Focus on figuring out what happened to make the other person perceive your actions as devaluing them. Can you determine why the other side feels dismissed, discounted, disenfranchised, disrespected, or disappointed? If you need help with this, consider switching roles and writing a letter to yourself as if you were the person on the other side.

Think about what the other person did to trigger this feeling in you. Define the "dissed" feeling that is fueling the conflict. Dismissed. Discounted. Disenfranchised. Disrespected. Disappointed.

Armed with this information, approach the conflict as an opportunity to improve your relationship, lessen tension, and eliminate any long-standing problems. If you feel confident that the person on the other side will be receptive to shining light onto the situation, you may decide to share your assessment with them. The goal will be to show them that your conflict is like a ping-pong game with the two of you sending the ball (represented by negatively perceived actions and communications) back and forth.

Once the conflict has been decoded—in that you are clear about how you co-created this mess—you will be able to treat the conflict as a natural part of the relationship. Once the core cause of the conflict has been exposed, you can move into brainstorming (tossing around ideas) and problem solving until a solution is reached and effective communication has been re-established.

Summary

At this point, you are on the road to quickly becoming a conflict expert. You now understand a lot about conflict dynamics, including the following:

➤ What conflict is, and how conflict plays out in our interpersonal relationships

➤ The physiological factors that drive our conflicts

➤ How you can calm your body and save yourself from conflict drama

In the next chapter, you will learn about the key issues that have the potential to cause significant workplace conflict, and how to keep them from damaging your career.

>2

Women at Work

In her book, *Lean In*, Facebook CEO Sheryl Sandberg recounted her own rise to the top and concluded that "as a man gets more successful, he is better liked by men and women, while as a woman gets more successful, she is less liked by men and women."

Statistics prove Sheryl is correct. Studies show that women are associated with nurturing qualities such as warmth, friendliness, and kindness. Men are associated with leadership qualities such as decisiveness, authoritativeness, and strength. When a woman fails to play along with the norm and displays the leadership qualities that are reserved for men, she is seen as unlikeable. In fact, successful women are likely to be perceived as aggressive, threatening, domineering, intimidating, abnormal, and unattractive. It's no wonder that many women have come to the conclusion that submission is mandatory if they want to be accepted.

In the U.S., men run roughly 97 percent of the largest public companies, hold 84 percent of major board positions, and control 83 percent of Congress. Truly powerful women remain a tiny minority, so it's so easy to stereotype them as ruthless and friendless. At the same time, women who display feminine traits are often judged as less competent and capable. So, in the workplace, many of us feel we are faced with a no-win situation: do we want to be viewed as competent or likeable?

In the past, ambitious women often used successful men as their role models. Many of these men were notoriously aggressive, propelled by the same killer instincts that their ancestors used to hunt or battle. Today, Sandberg and many other influential women are paving a different path. Women are realizing that they don't have to be "men in skirts." Instead, we can secure respect by coupling our feminine natures with presence and confidence.

The gap between men and women in politics and business is slowly continuing to shrink. With time, the old images and stereotypes may even disappear. In the meantime, this section will help you make your way in the workplace. In this chapter, you will learn the following:

- ➤ How and why men and women react differently to conflict
- ➤ Ways women operate (and work) differently than men
- ➤ How to get the best out of a business partnership
- ➤ What you need to know to ensure that a workplace friendship or romance doesn't damage your career

Women and the new workplace

A generation ago, the workplace was gender segregated, with gender determining a large part of each worker's options. While many of these restrictions have been lifted, we are still gendered individuals with organizational and relational histories. We bring these histories into the workplace where they can cause tension.

Women, men, and conflict behaviors

Girls frequently engage in one-on-one play, avoiding the team sports that teach boys to play with their enemies and against their friends. Influenced by a combination of adaptive biological survival mechanisms and social influences, these childhood gender differences continue throughout the lifespan.

We know that social norms, culture, and individual differences regulate aggressive behavior. Research has shown that males are more likely than females to use physical and verbal aggression when faced with conflict. On the other hand, females are more likely to use indirect aggression such as gossip, rumor-spreading, and undermining by enlisting the cooperation of a third party.

Recent research at UCLA has found another interesting difference between men and women and how they respond to threat. As you will remember from *Chapter 1, All About Conflict*, the fight-or-flight response is a physiological response connected to a variety of bodily symptoms. Additionally it is a behavioral response. The behaviors (fighting or fleeing) can be observed in humans and other animals when there is a perceived threat. However, UCLA researchers have found that females (human and other animals) also exhibit another behavioral response to threat. Considering the limits of female physical strength (fight) and the ability to run with small children (flight), it makes sense that females have had to adapt and find more fitting ways to deal with threat. This evolutionary adaptation has been termed "**tend and befriend**." Tending is about nurturing and protecting. Befriending is about connecting to a social group in order to reduce risk and manage threats or stressful conditions. You can find the published study at http://taylorlab.psych.ucla.edu.

Case study

Christine, a teacher, says that all of her coworkers are women. This is how she described her workplace conflict management strategy:

> *"Women love to gossip and talk about one another. Unfortunately, many women talk behind each other's backs. I have learned to be silent during these conversations at work. I try NOT to comment. Instead, I just listen. Also, I NEVER mention or repeat what I have heard about others. This is the way that I avoid workplace drama."*

Christine is wise. What she does is to demonstrate her trustworthiness so that other women feel safe coming to her when they are feeling threatened or angry. This is a great example of "tend and befriend." Please follow Christine's example and learn to hold your comments. This is the most valuable conflict-management strategy you can employ.

Evelyn, an attorney, has figured out that she has to change strategies depending on the gender of the lawyer on the other side. She says:

"Typically, when my opposition is a man, I play along and go with strategies that range from a dumb blonde, to a wise mother, to one of the boys who's in on the joke. When the opposition is a woman, I approach her as a fellow comrade-in-arms, on equal footing, and befriend her, while trying to gain an advantage."

The "tend and befriend" researchers at UCLA found that under stress conditions, females had an enhanced desire for social contact. As similar behavior has been observed in monkeys, rats, and other animals, they believe that "tend and befriend" is a behavioral response as opposed to a social role.

However, *if women want to "play" in the workplace, we will need to become comfortable with some of the conflict-management strategies men learned as children,* as well as the strategies we learned as children.

During the 1960s and 70s, Swiss psychologist Jean Piaget studied the nature and development of human intelligence. One of Piaget's conclusions was that the games girls prefer do not have the same complex or rigid rules systems as the games that boys favor. Piaget found girls less concerned with rules, more ready to relax them, and more concerned about cooperation, innovation, and tolerance. There is, however, some disagreement about the interpretation of Piaget's findings. Some developmental psychologists say that Piaget concluded that girls' limited interest in rules pointed to a slower moral (right versus wrong) maturity. Others believe that Piaget regarded girls' desire to work together as evidence of girls' moral advancement.

Considering what we now know about the female "tend and befriend" behavioral response to threat, it makes sense that girls are more concerned with relationship building and less concerned with laws and rules. During the last decade, MRIs and other brain-imaging tools have allowed neuroscience researchers to identify structural and functional differences between male and female brains. Many of these differences start in the womb. Here are some of the things we now know:

> ➤ Men are more likely to be left-brain dominant, while women tend to be more evenly balanced between left and right brain processing. Women are therefore more intuitive, while men, who are more task oriented, may have trouble picking up on emotional cues unless they are clearly verbalized.

> ➤ The inferior-parietal lobule, which controls numerical brain function, is larger in men than in women. This explains why men score higher on mathematical tests than women.

> ➤ Two brain areas that deal with language are larger in women. Women process language in both brain hemispheres, while men use only one.

> ➤ As women have larger limbic systems than men, women are typically better able to express their emotions and connect with others. However, women are also more prone to different types of depression.

> ➤ The parietal region is thicker in the female brain, making spatial tasks harder for women.

Business partnerships

Women are starting new businesses in record numbers. Many of these new women business owners find that partnership is a comfortable format and they are turning to their family members, spouses, coworkers, friends, as well as "unknowns" when they seek out business partners. This section will teach you the success strategies business partners need to know.

Team sports prepare boys for the corporate model of business. Girls, however, typically play closely with one or two friends. This one-on-one play is great preparation for entrepreneurial partnership. So, it is fitting that many women find partnership a comfortable business format. Partnership works for women coming from a wide range of backgrounds and experiences including those tired of hitting the corporate glass ceiling, stay-at-home moms, and women who want to turn their passions and social connections into business ideas.

Partnership brings a wide variety of benefits, including a sense of connection and someone to cover when you go on vacation. On the other hand, many partnerships end in crisis and conflict. To avoid partnership failure, your partnership needs to possess the following seven components of positive partnership.

Shared values

Partners need a sense of shared standards regarding what is desirable, undesirable, good, and bad. These values will guide partners' actions, judgments, and choices. Values, which often carry considerable emotion, may range from valuing family, prosperity, ambition, a work ethic, or a political persuasion. In addition to helping partners make congruent decisions, shared values serve to keep partners united (see the values self-assessment at the end of *Chapter 3, Workplace Conflict in the New Normal – The Reasons and the Costs*).

Complementary skills and traits

Successful partners will possess different (complementary) skills and traits. The broader the partners' range of skills, the clearer the division of their labor (and power) can be. It may be easy to distinguish the marketing person from the technical person in a business, but other necessary variables are often not as easy to see. Michael Gerber's classic book, *The E-Myth,* explains that a business owner needs to play three roles: entrepreneur (the creative visionary), manager (the administrator who brings planning, order, and predictability), and technician (the craftsperson). Partnerships have a distinct advantage in that two or more invested people are available to contribute to performing the three necessary roles.

Sense of equity

Equity occurs when each person in a relationship believes that the rewards they are receiving are proportional to their contributions. Strangers and casual acquaintances maintain equity by keeping track of the benefits they exchange. However, in long-term and more committed relationships, it is not healthy to keep track. Instead, a sense of equity should be established. A perception of inequity (I am giving more then I get) takes a tremendous toll on a partnership.

Growing together

From the moment we are born until the day we die, we are in the process of growing and changing. Partners and their partnerships are continuously undergoing this process of change. However, we are often not aware of the changes we're experiencing. Sometimes, change is viewed as a threat to the status quo. Successful partners embrace change and growth, knowing that this attitude benefits both their individual and shared professional identities.

Proactive conflict management strategies

Competing and avoiding are not effective conflict-management strategies for business partners to use with one another. Instead, successful partners use proactive and strategic conflict management approaches such as accommodation, compromise, and collaboration to resolve their differences.

Shared vision

Partners need a shared vision or plan for the future. Vision is what determines and expresses where an organization wants to go and how it intends to get there. A shared vision allows partners to focus on their goals and the methods they will use to achieve those goals. When partners hold different visions, they become discouraged, overwhelmed, and disconnected. In order to create and effectively benefit from a shared vision, four tasks are necessary: creating the initial vision, translating that vision into the necessary physical actions, articulating and selling the vision to others, and holding true to the essence of the vision when reality changes the plans (see the visioning self-assessment at the end of *Chapter 3, Workplace Conflict in the New Normal – The Reasons and the Costs*).

An exit strategy

It has been said that a graceful exit is proof of a successful venture. Without an exit strategy in place, partners can be faced with making crucial decisions at a time when they are least levelheaded. An exit strategy is a shared sense of when and how an alliance will end, and should always be included as the endpoint in a business plan. However, while planning for the end may be a critical aspect of owning a business, it is also one of the most neglected. Exits are easy to avoid when the issue is not pressing, and raising the issue might sour the deal or suggest a lack of trust. You should address these four questions when considering an exit plan:

List

What events might trigger an end to the partnership?

How will the business be valued at the end?

Which options for future ownership are acceptable?

What post-alliance ties and restrictions, such as noncompete clauses, need to be included?

When you enter into a partnership that is strong in these seven components, you have the potential to create synergy and reap some amazing benefits. True synergy comes about when two (or more) people work together to create results that would have been unobtainable independently. In a synergistic partnership, *2+2>4*, and the whole is greater than the sum of its parts.

However, let me leave you here with a word of caution. Business ownership, typically, will bring about a change in the relationship you and your partner shared prior to starting your business. This change can be either positive or negative. Additionally, starting out with a strong connection may lead a business' founding team to rely more on unspoken agreements and less on written contracts. Of course, it is better to discuss thorny issues while you and your partners are still within the window of venture enthusiasm and working friendship. However, often, no one wants to shake up the honeymoon, and difficult issues may be sidestepped and only addressed when the team has begun to encounter operational problems. Do not fall into this trap.

Action Point

If you do not talk to your partner about uncomfortable subjects when all is well, it will be torture to have to do it later when you hit the inevitable bumps on the road. Practice having those difficult discussions now.

Friendship at work

Women tend to make friends at work. It's part of our biology. Earlier, we discussed research at UCLA which found that females (humans and other animals) are apt to respond to a threat with a behavioral response that the researchers termed "tend and befriend." When we use this evolutionary adaptation, the goal is to connect to a social group and reduce risk.

We are living in an increasingly mobile society. "Till-death-do-us-part" marriages are becoming rare. Many of us can no longer depend on our extended families for social support. Where do we turn to fill in the gaps? Our friends. For busy professional women, work is often where our friends are. Workplace friendships can provide big benefits as well as pose some serious pitfalls. This section will teach you what you need to know to ensure that a business friendship doesn't damage your career.

Sometimes, we meet friends at work, befriending the boss, a coworker, or an employee. Sometimes, we hire our friends into our workplaces. Sometimes, we go into business with our friends. In any event, adding a layer of friendship onto a business relationship can bring both benefits and the potential for disaster.

Work friends are easily accessible. Together for long periods of time, we typically share interests, experiences, a professional identity, and a common history. These friends can listen, console, advise, teach, share, and support. So, a workplace friendship can often provide you with an improved understanding of your world and yourself. Whether the friend is one you hired into the workplace or one you met at work, friendship often brings team strength, more efficient decision making, and effective conflict management. For women, especially, friendship can create a supportive business culture that discourages political behavior and promotes candor, self-disclosure, communication, tolerance, and cooperation. Friendship may bring involvement and commitment to the workplace that would not exist otherwise. Ultimately, good working relationships and good friendships are characterized by shared goals and close contact. So, friendship, which is typically associated with similarity of values, is a great foundation for workplace connections and joint decision making.

On the other hand, a workplace friendship can be detrimental to a career. Intimate sharing and excessive disclosure to a coworker can come back and bite you on the nose. Likewise, making decisions based on friendship—ignoring what is best for the business or your career—can be professional suicide. A soured friendship can spill over into the workplace, causing disruption and distraction. Friends who are very involved with one another inside and outside of work often have a more trusting relationship. However, this close involvement may also invite severe interpersonal conflict that brings the potential to provoke an ugly end to the relationship. The bonds of friendship can serve to keep you or your friend connected to your business, even if this means passing up more attractive opportunities.

Ultimately, workplace friends may be what is best about work and what is worst about work. Be careful. As close as you two may be, when push comes to shove, if your friend has to choose between the hand that feeds her (the boss) and you, she is likely to throw you under the bus.

Romance at work

We have all heard stories of women who used sexual power to get what they wanted at work. On the other hand, women often allow romantic desires to damage their careers. Clearly, sexual and romantic activities at work can bite you on the nose. So, tread lightly if you decide to sleep with the boss or a coworker. Most importantly, *keep the details of your trysts to yourself.* While you may feel driven to share what is going on with your best workplace friend, no good can come from this disclosure. As safe as your friend might feel, the revelation of your sexual activity will change the dynamics between you. The gossip may be too juicy for her to keep to herself, no matter how loyal she has been in the past. So, if you have to do it, keep it to yourself.

Self-assessment

When you have time to sit and reflect, answer the following questions:

- ➤ What lessons did you learn from your father about work?
- ➤ What lessons did you learn from your mother about work?
- ➤ What is your greatest work-related strength?
- ➤ What is your work-related challenge that is most difficult to overcome?
- ➤ What is the worst mistake you ever made at work?
- ➤ Motivational speaker Jim Rohn professed, "You are the average of the five people you spend the most time with." Who are the five people you spend the most time with? What steps are you willing to take to improve your life by revising this list?

Summary

While men are inclined to focus on problems and tasks, women are likely to get involved with other people's feelings and stories. This relational style presents women with unique challenges and benefits in the workplace. To help you sort it all out and make your way in the workplace, this chapter taught you the following:

- ➤ The impact gender has on our threat responses
- ➤ The components of a successful business partnership, and how to keep it that way
- ➤ How to ensure that a business friendship or a workplace romance doesn't damage your career

Certainly, all men are not alike, and all women are not alike. However, in general, women operate (and work) differently than men. You can be most effective when you consider these differences in your workplace interactions.

In the next chapter, we'll uncover the hidden causes and costs of modern day workplace conflicts and dive into the advanced strategies to deal with them.

>3

Workplace Conflict in the New Normal – The Reasons and the Costs

We are living in an era of incredible, unprecedented change. Every aspect of how we work and who does what in the field, factory, farm, and office has felt the effects of change. These changes—the new economy, evolving gender roles, global competition, technological advances, and heightened security concerns—have increased the potential for conflict in your workplace.

In *Chapter 1, All About Conflict*, you learned that our workplace conflicts are triggered by a physiological **fight-or-flight survival response.** In addition, we discussed how *inconsistent or incompatible expectations* between individuals or groups can drive our conflicts. Along with these interpersonal dynamics, when a workplace conflict erupts, there are usually other factors involved. Typically, environmental, situational, or circumstantial factors are also at play. In this chapter, we will look more closely at those aspects of workplace conflict.

At the end of this chapter, you will understand the following:

> ➤ The toll workplace conflict can take on your organization and your career

> ➤ How the realities of the new workplace set you up for conflict

> ➤ How to identify and overcome differences in communication, management style, power dynamics, core values, and life vision

The costs of workplace conflict

In the workplace, even minor arguments and disputes can take a toll on individual careers, personal health, relationships, teamwork, and overall productivity. Conflict can sour the climate of the organization, undermine morale, interfere with performance, or erupt into dangerous and violent confrontations. Ultimately, conflicts can cause loyal, valuable employees to become alienated, forcing voluntary or involuntary terminations.

Coworker flare-ups may sound petty, but they can have disastrous consequences. An angry employee can destroy team morale, create anxiety among coworkers, engage in sabotage, or become so enraged that they spark a violent outburst. When the air between two people (or two teams) is no longer clear, the "smog" can greatly reduce the quality of their communication, create negative feelings, and generate further resentments.

Sometimes, the symptoms of conflict are obvious with an employee who is shouting, slamming doors, crying, and so on. Sometimes, they are more subtle, as with a person who displays no desire to communicate, sulks, slows down, frequently calls in sick, or has repeated accidents. Some people will use obvious addictions such as food, alcohol, gambling, or drugs to become less conscious and numb their sense of threat. Some people will use harder-to-detect layers of avoidance such as silence or smiling. If these conflict symptoms are not acknowledged and dealt with, more and more tension can pile up until a slight stimulant, such as an offhand word, causes a major eruption.

When someone is unable or unwilling to deal with confrontation head-on, they may spend time building a case; assemble others in the organization to their side; create insulting or degrading graffiti; engage in vandalism; spread rumors, harass, stalk, or make terrorist threats; and refuse to cooperate, share information, or work. You can imagine how these behaviors can take their toll on an organization and the people in it. In the end, the longer the confrontation is avoided, the more likely it is that people in the organization will become aware of the tension. Ultimately, the entire system may be affected.

Various studies from the fields of management and human resources maintain that supervisors and managers spend 18-25 percent of their time on conflict management. While it's just about impossible to create an accurate cost analysis detailing what conflict really costs you or your organization, we can estimate that your company is likely spending $12,000 of a manager's $60,000 yearly salary on conflict resolution. Additionally, costs in production, employee turnover, sick time, and conflict-related absenteeism take an additional toll. The cost of defending a wrongful dismissal, sexual harassment, discrimination, or similar claim can be astronomical. The potential costs resulting from the trauma and harm of negative press from such a claim can be exorbitant.

The reasons for workplace conflict

Rapid pace and constant change are characteristic of the modern workplace. The changes that have the most conflict-producing potential include the following:

> ➤ Advances in technology that have created new jobs, while destroying old ones. The result is an army of workers that are unprepared and afraid of the future.

- ➤ Global competition and collaboration, which serves as a motive to cut labor costs. Typically, this striving for reduced labor costs results in lessened job security, which ultimately leads to lessened worker loyalty.

- ➤ Increased participation and presence of women and people of varied races, ethnic backgrounds, and cultures in workplaces that were previously more homogeneous or segregated. Without yesteryear's clearly defined roles and divisions of labor, our workplaces are ripe for misunderstandings and abuses of power.

- ➤ Frequent restructuring and multiple mergers that leave workers vying for positions in "step-families" where the fear of being redundant reigns and organizational charts make no sense.

- ➤ Easy and frequent access to unverified information.

- ➤ Diminished access to credit coupled with a reorganizing real-estate market.

- ➤ A farewell to the concept of an upwardly mobile society.

- ➤ Cell phones and tablets that create expectations for immediate responses.

As a result of these changes, it is likely that sometime in your career, you will encounter some version of the following:

- ➤ Competition that has gotten out of control
- ➤ Intolerance, prejudice, discrimination, or bigotry
- ➤ Perceived inequities
- ➤ Misunderstandings
- ➤ Gossip, rumors, and falsehoods
- ➤ Long-standing grudges or misplaced loyalties
- ➤ Job insecurity or a sense of having been bypassed for a promotion
- ➤ A perception of reputation and identity being at stake
- ➤ Sexual tensions or harassment
- ➤ A perceived threat to security, power, or status
- ➤ Workplace romance gone awry
- ➤ Comparisons of performance ratings or bonuses
- ➤ A pattern of blaming others for mistakes
- ➤ Alcohol- or drug-induced irrational behaviors
- ➤ Conflicts relating to employment terms or job tasks
- ➤ Office or organizational politics
- ➤ Juggling for status, influence, security, respect, and rank
- ➤ Individual agendas and conflicting responsibilities that outweigh the mandate to collaborate
- ➤ Working for long hours in close quarters, with a lack of resources
- ➤ Strong allegiances to subgroups (for example, the department, the union, a professional identity, management, and so on)

> Feeling wronged, misunderstood, or unheard

> Cyber bullying, cyber stalking, and privacy disputes

> Misunderstandings based on gender, age, race, and/or cultural differences. (In addition to the effect of gender on our communication or conversational styles, when speakers from different parts of the country or from different ethnic or class backgrounds talk to each other, it is likely that their words will not be understood exactly as they were intended.)

You may find yourself dealing with these issues directly. Alternatively, you might be in the role of supervisor, on-looking coworker, or stuck-in-the-middle mediator. In any event, your best course of action is usually to start off by defining all of the issues that are lurking under a conflict, including the individual (for example, feeling dismissed or devalued), the interpersonal (for example, a cultural difference), and the situational or environmental (for example, a recent budget cut).

Let's delve into the five overarching factors that are responsible for a lot of the heat in a conflict-charged environment: differences in communication style, management style, power, values, and vision.

Communication differences

We are either **direct communicators**, also called **pointers** (who want to get to the point), or **indirect communicators**, also called **painters** (who want to paint a picture). Direct communicators (the pointers) see talking as a means of *trading information*. Indirect or relational communicators (the painters) see talking as a way of *connecting*. Both pointers and painters will frequently find the other style irritating. Difficulties arise in the workplace when pointers and painters fail to find balance between their two styles and instead allow their conversations to turn into a series of misinterpretations.

Make a note

When you are dealing with a painter/pointer situation, there is hope. If you are directly involved, try to alter your style so that your message is not lost. If you are indirectly involved, serving in an intermediary role between two other people, explain the pointer-painter concept and ask them if they can see how it fits their situation. Remember, neither style is right or wrong. Most of us fall somewhere along a pointer-painter continuum, and we can comfortably use both styles. With just a little insight, it is almost always possible to find common ground.

In her book, *You Just Don't Understand: Women and Men in Conversation*, communications expert Deborah Tannen says that "talk between men and women is cross-cultural communication", because "girls and boys grow up in different worlds of words." Men's language often reflects the fact that men see themselves as problem solvers. This problem-solving focus can be interpreted as domineering by a woman who wants to build rapport. For more details on her work refer to http://www.georgetown.edu/faculty/tannend/index.html.

Women can talk to other women in ways that they cannot talk to men. Men can talk to other men in ways that they cannot talk to women. Keep in mind that the high comfort level we often experience with same-gender communications may be used to bypass status lines and workplace hierarchies.

Communication tips

If you want to be believed, your tone of voice and body language must be in agreement with your words. Others will believe your tone and your nonverbal messages, as opposed to your words, if there is inconsistency between them. This is one of the reasons why it's especially difficult to effectively communicate when emotions are strong. However, if you follow these communication tips, you can get through almost anything.

Action Point

Frustration can best be understood as the feeling of waiting behind another car at a green light. You just want them to move—now! When someone you are dealing with is feeling this frustration, it is best to validate the feeling and give them a way out of it. Start with "I understand your frustration. In order to help you, I need…"

Never tell someone who is agitated to "calm down." When we are upset, we usually believe that the problem is external. Telling someone to calm down tells them "you are the problem," and this is the last thing they want to hear. Instead, start off with "Let's both stay calm. I will do whatever I can to fix this problem."

Avoid trading insults or nastiness

Avoid formulas such as "have a nice day," and "thank you for shopping at XYZ department store." Formulas tend to become singsong and insincere.

Use this set of questions to guide a discussion under stress:

- Where are we now?
- Where do we want to be?
- How will we get there?
- What do you need to do?
- How can I help?

Suggest a delay so that people can cool off, think, and process information. Sometimes, all that's necessary is a few minutes, but a few hours or days may be the best prescription.

Before you respond with "but", consider using "and" instead.

Frame workplace disputes as mutual problems. Separate the people from the problem by laying out the facts and then asking "how can we resolve this?"

Don't waste energy asking someone else to change. It's difficult to change when we are highly motivated. It's almost impossible to change when the impetus for change is coming from an external force.

Management styles

Some workplace conflicts are the result of management style or inappropriate management behavior. Managers who fail to support employees, do not follow through on promises and tasks, or fail to take charge passively encourage conflicts. Certainly, no manager should ever ridicule, embarrass, talk down to, or hurt employees. However, the absence of these negative behaviors is not enough. Employee expectations have changed considerably over the past decade. Now more than ever, employees want flexibility (for example, the ability to work from home) to know that their input is valued, and that they are making an important contribution. Ultimately, some workers want balance between their careers and personal lives while others want to maximize their professional growth.

Make a note

Successful managers grow into their own management styles. However, *effective management always involves employees who feel valued and a part of the team.* Without this, your workplace will be ripe for conflict, high turnover, and decreased productivity.

If you are in the managerial position, do all you can to convey to your employees that you value them. Encourage them. Give them space to figure things out on their own. Be there as a backup, waiting in the wings if they need you. To a great extent, management is about creating a legacy. It is one way we have to influence the future. Your employees will remember you. While they may not be able to remember your title, they will remember how you made them feel.

Power – personal, positional, and perception

Power is a component of our social relationships. Anytime two people depend on one another, power is involved. As almost every conflict involves some level of power imbalance, understanding power is critical to understanding conflict management.

In his book, *David and Goliath*, Malcolm Gladwell explains that the famous "duel revels the folly of our assumptions about power" and shows us that power can come in many forms: "in breaking rules, and in substituting speed and surprise for strength." Gladwell is correct; there are a wide variety of definitions and distinctions about kinds of power. It's easy to fall into a trap and see our limitations while we forget about our less-obvious strengths. When you are trying to assess how power is affecting a conflict in your workplace, the first thing to do is consider if the power that each person is exercising is best classified as **power-over** (which is linked to coercion, control, and dominance) or **power-to** (the ability to act, influence, and say no). Additionally, you will want to look at the *source of power.* Typically, all sources of power can be sorted into two categories: **positional power**, which comes from position or rank, and **personal power**, which emanates from a person's individual characteristics.

The six sources of power

Social psychologists have identified six sources or bases of power. They are as follows:

- ➤ Reward power
- ➤ Coercive power
- ➤ Legitimate power
- ➤ Expert power
- ➤ Informational power
- ➤ Referent power

Reward power, coercive power, and legitimate power are forms of positional power. Expert power, informational power, and referent power are forms of personal power.

Reward power

Reward power involves giving rewards or taking away unwanted things or conditions. When you have the ability to offer raises or promotions, you have reward power. The problem with reward power is that when you use up the available rewards or the rewards don't have enough perceived value, your power weakens.

Coercive power

Coercive power, which includes the power to punish, is about force and threats. There is little room for coercive power in the workplace.

Legitimate power

Legitimate power is rooted in one's position, rank, or title. People will usually obey the person in charge. The weakness of legitimate power is that it is lost when positions change.

Expert power

Expert power comes from a person's perceived experience, knowledge, or ability. Doctors and lawyers have expert power.

Informational power

Informational power is based on the power holder's potential to use or share information to help or persuade others.

Referent power

Referent power comes from personal qualities. Politicians, celebrities, and admired role models often have referent power. This form of power is especially strong when it is combined with another form of power.

In a workplace dispute, power often seesaws. A supervisor or manager may have positional or personal power. However, an employee can have referent power and informational power that they use to organize a mutiny or polarize the workplace into factions.

Power-balancing techniques

Use these power-balancing techniques to help lessen the power imbalances you encounter:

List

Limit the power of the high-power party. Of course, this means the high-power party has to be willing to go along with the plan. What's in it for them? They might know that this is their only opportunity to learn what is really going on. Agreeing up front not to act on the revealed information allows the low-power party to share without fear of reprisal.

Focus on interdependence. This can be done by listing ways the people involved can help one another. The people involved may find surprising answers to the key questions of "What's in it for me?", "What are you willing to give?", and "What do you want?"

Persist in a calm manner. The woman who loses her cool loses her power. When someone becomes agitated in response to another person's words or actions, they are allowing an outside force to dictate their behavior. Think about it. If worker A is able to push worker B's buttons and get B to react, then A is in charge. If instead, B calmly persists, A no longer has control of B's physiology.

Speak up for your own worth and outline your contributions and assets. Hopefully, when you are speaking, the other person is listening. However, even if they aren't, you are. Verbalize your value. You may just surprise yourself at how wonderful you are. Knowing that will give you power, even when you are faced with the most powerful adversary.

Meta-communicate. Meta-communicating is communicating about how you are communicating. If someone is abusing their power, using bully tactics, or dirty negotiation strategies, you may choose to discuss how their communication strategies are affecting your interactions.

Core value differences

Your core values represent the essence of what is most important in your life. These values define what brings you personal and professional fulfillment. When you are conscious of your values, they will serve as your internal compass. Just like the compass needle points to the magnetic North pole, your values can guide you in the right direction when you follow their pull. Being able to orient your work and your life around your core values can provide inspiration and satisfaction. On the other hand, values' misalignment is often at the root of draining obligations, boredom, confusion, tension, and frustration.

Self-assessment – your values

When you have time to sit and reflect, this exercise will help you clarify your core values.

Action Point

Slowly read the words below and circle the words that you feel drawn to. Needless to say, there are no correct or incorrect answers. There is some space for your own words if you find that one is missing from the list.

Family	Generosity	Competing/winning	Honoring of self
Wisdom	Friendship	Health	Freedom
Advancement	Spirituality	Affection	Cooperation
Loyalty	Culture	Responsibility	Adventure
Inner peace	Order	Achievement	Involvement
Structure	Wealth	Creativity	Influence
Pleasure	Excellence	Independence	Inspiration
Connection	Community	Power	Peace
Intimacy	Integrity	Beauty	Belonging
Support	Knowledge	Education	Serenity
Purpose	Love	Companionship	Accomplishment
Financial security	Recognition	Social change	Personal development
Legacy	Attractiveness	Passion	Perseverance
Enlightenment	Having fun	Self-improvement	Honesty
Ingenuity	Moving forward	Originality	Sensuality
Service	Compassion	Strength	Tenderness
The unknown	Thrills	Contributing	Experience
Imagination	Religion	Persistence	Resourcefulness
Punctuality	Honesty	Consistency	Commitment
Work ethic	_____	_____	_____

Go back through your list and choose your top five. Mark these values with a checkmark.

These are your core values, representing what matters most to you and what you really want in your life. Write down your core values, and for each one, ask yourself:

Action Point

What does this value mean to me?

Why is it important?

Which of my activities and commitments express this core value?

Which of my core values are expressed in my work?

Which areas of my life are most aligned with my core values?

Which of my values need more expression?

This week, notice how your core values are expressed in the decisions you make. Are you expressing your values and adjusting your work and life around them? Or, on the other hand, are you living with value misalignment? You can gauge this by looking at your calendar and checkbook. The goal is to choose to spend your time and money in ways that reflect your values.

Finally, keep in mind that your values are just yours. The people you work with do not share all of your values. Accepting and embracing these value differences is part of good conflict management and a way to make life easier.

Vision clashes

Your vision is your plan for your future. It is the picture of your future that begins in your imagination. Your vision allows you to focus on capturing, communicating, and reconciling your goals and your methods to achieve those goals. Ultimately, your life vision serves as reinforcement, as it increases your clarity, enthusiasm, and commitment. Knowing where you're going and how you intend to get there will contribute to the self-direction and drive that are necessary for your success.

Self-assessment – your life vision

The following are the steps for self-assessment:

Step 1 – clarify your vision

Your willingness and ability to envision are the keys to your creating a life vision. Envisioning is about dreaming. Close your eyes, take a few deep breaths, and give yourself permission to relax. Gently, without judgments, fast forward your life one year into the future. Good news! You are living your perfect life! Let your mind run free—there are no restrictions in your perfect life. Focus on where you are, on what is happening, who you are with, and how you are feeling. Allow yourself to see as much detail as possible. When you are clear about your vision, begin to write using the following questions as a guide:

List

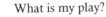

Where am I?

What am I doing?

What is my work?

What is my play?

What is different about me, my situation, and/or my environment?

What is the same?

What have I accomplished?

Who is with me?

Who is no longer in my life?

Is there anything else worth noting?

Step 2 – live your vision

Step into your vision and stay there. Act "as if." Observe how this feels. As you step into your vision, you align yourself with the life that is waiting for you.

Make a note

Often, conflict at work is ignited when someone believes that their vision cannot coexist with the vision of a coworker or supervisor. When you are faced with a workplace conflict, think about how your vision and the vision of the other person can be in alignment.

You will see how values and vision can help you get to the root of a conflict in *Chapter 6, Conflict Conversations*.

Summary

Since work often provides food, clothing, shelter, medical care, status, security, and a variety of other benefits, it is not surprising that a perception of threat to workplace security can trigger strong emotions. The likely method of releasing these strong emotions may be a volcanic eruption that serves no one. Thankfully, you won't be the one erupting because you now know that:

> Individual, interpersonal, and environmental factors drive workplace conflict

> Workplace conflict can impose significant costs on your career and your organization

> Personal and positional power dynamics and power-balancing strategies can be used to overcome a power disadvantage

You have also learned:

> ➤ How to define your core values, and how value misalignment can cause conflict

> ➤ How to access your life vision and how envisioning can motivate you to reach your full potential

In the next chapter, you will learn how to use specific negotiation styles and conflict-management methods to your advantage.

Conflict Management Styles, Strategies, and Methods

When stress is high, having a grasp on a conflict-management framework is a key way to stay on task. This framework should include strategies you use individually as well as familiarity with a variety of available methods or processes.

What do you typically do when you are faced with conflict? Do you tend to avoid conflicts or face each one head-on, never taking no for an answer? Or is your usual response to conflict somewhere between these two extremes? Do you handle (or mishandle) all your conflicts the same way, or are you one person with your spouse and another at work?

Frequently, workplace, family, and community conflicts cannot be *permanently* resolved. Instead, the best strategy is to manage them. In the preface, I explained that "manage" in "conflict management" doesn't mean control; it means "to care for," like you manage your investments, or "to handle," as in, "her husband managed while she was out of town." We each have our own style for dealing with conflict. However, researchers have identified five basic styles or strategies that are commonly used in response to conflict. These are also considered the five basic negotiation strategies and are used to negotiate everything from where to go for lunch to complex salary negotiations. At the end of this chapter, you will understand the following:

> ➤ The five conflict-management styles: avoid, accommodate, combat, compromise, and collaborate

> ➤ Seven conflict-management methods: insight, negotiation, facilitation, mediation, arbitration, litigation, and unilateral decision-making power

What's your style?

Effective conflict managers use different conflict-management (and negotiation) strategies or styles depending on their goals and their relationship to the person on the other side. When we are able to choose the most appropriate style or strategy, we are able to turn conflicts into positive growth, engage in brainstorming, improve relationships, lessen tension, and eliminate long-standing problems. However, each of us has natural style preferences, just like we each prefer to use our right hand or left hand. Knowing your conflict-management preference will allow you to move beyond it and choose the most effective style for any given situation.

The five styles or strategies that are commonly used in response to conflict as well as to negotiate are as follows:

- **Avoid**: The ostrich that bolts, withdraws, and retreats. "Whatever! I'll just leave my marbles and go home when no one is looking."

- **Accommodate**: The doormat that concedes, allows, and appeases. "You can play with my marbles. Here, they're yours."

- **Combat**: The ass-kicker who controls, competes, and forces. "I will get your marbles even if I have to lie, cheat, and steal to make it happen."

- **Compromise**: The equalizer who seeks middle ground, a fair exchange, and to share and share alike. "Let's share our marbles. Can we cut them all in half?"

- **Collaborate**: The problem solver who questions, analyzes, and joins forces. "Let's talk about some ways to get this marble thing working for both of us. Can you tell me your vision for the marbles?"

It is critical that you are familiar and comfortable with each style so that you can select the strategy that best meets your desired outcome.

We can look at each of these styles with two priorities in mind: **achieving goals** and **building relationships**. Achieving goals is about getting what you want or satisfying your personal agenda. Relationship building is about preserving or improving the relationship with the person on the other side. Each style has strengths and weaknesses and can be effective at certain times, in certain situations, and with certain people:

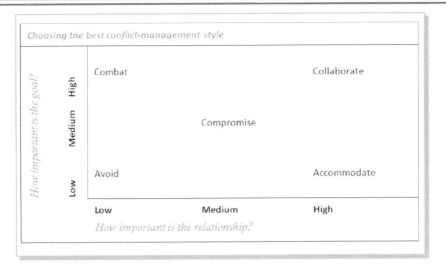

Avoid – the ostrich

In the face of conflict, the ostrich avoids, bolts, withdraws, and retreats. People who are comfortable with avoidance often see conflict as futile. They withdraw without satisfying their own goals or improving the relationship with the person on the other side. Ultimately, avoiders leave solutions to chance, and they usually prefer to pay the price rather than face the conflict.

Avoiding is a good strategy to use when:

> There is nothing significant to be gained from the conflict

> The relationship with the person on the other side is insignificant

> The person on the other side has a totally different agenda that does not compete with yours

> Your priority is to get away

> You believe that your opponent might be dangerous

> You are terminating this relationship or otherwise becoming independent of one another

> You will benefit from a cooling-off period

> You need a temporary solution in order to buy time, gather information, or prepare your plan B

> The issue or issues involved are minor

> Your preferred outcome is impossible or unrealistic

> There has already been a determination that the other party is right or that they are going to triumph no matter what you do

When this strategy is misused, important goals and relationships are put at risk. In your personal life and in the current business environment where success is often based on on-going relationships, avoiding is usually a bad choice. Ultimately, if you're a chronic avoider, leaving solutions to chance, your frustrated friends, business associates, and family members will label you a poor communicator. It's easy to fall into the avoiding trap if you have been programmed since childhood not to rock the boat. If that's you, make a conscious effort to regularly avoid avoiding.

Accommodate – the doormat

In the face of conflict, the doormat concedes, allows, appeases, smoothes, suppresses, and calms others. Occasionally, we should all be willing to accommodate. You can buy a lot of loyalty with your personal and professional connections by accommodating simple requests. On the other hand, if you consistently accommodate when you don't want to or when it doesn't serve you, you will ultimately wind up feeling victimized and abused. While you might be able to play the martyr for a little while, others will soon see that you are the only one responsible for your abuse.

Accommodating is a good strategy to use when:

> Your goal is to maintain a relationship or please the other side

> Maintaining a relationship is more important than the issues in question

> You are sure that you cannot maintain the relationship while achieving your personal goal

> You want to cover up, minimize differences, or pretend that everything is OK

> You want to pacify the other party or create the illusion of a calm and harmonious atmosphere

> You need a temporary solution in order to buy time, gather information, or prepare your plan B

> The issue or issues involved are minor

> A disruption in the relationship would be damaging

> There has already been a determination that the other party is right or that they are going to triumph no matter what you do

> The other side might be dangerous

When this strategy is misused, it involves constant pacifying, covering up, pretending everything is OK, minimizing differences, and abandoning one's own needs and desires in order to meet another's requests or demands. If you are a chronic accommodator, you have probably found that the self-destructive pattern of excessive giving leaves you feeling resentful and disappointed.

Combat – the ass-kicker

In the face of conflict, the ass-kicker controls, competes, and forces. People who are comfortable with competition fight their battles, seeking to win. They believe that a clear winner and a clear loser will always emerge so they keep the focus on achieving their personal goals and show less concern for relationships. Typically, this strong desire to achieve is coupled with the use of force, hidden activities, or power.

Combating is a good strategy to use when:

> ➤ Winning is the goal, and winning is more important than the relationship with the person on the other side

> ➤ The issue or issues at hand are extremely important

> ➤ Giving in would result in tremendous loss

> ➤ Your opponent is unwilling to accept anything short of a total win

> ➤ Action is urgently required

> ➤ Only one side can achieve their desired outcome

Combating may help you achieve your goal, but this strategy should be used with caution in the workplace and at home. The perception that you are a steamroller can make you seem unsafe or controlling. Use this strategy sparingly with those you love or when you care about bolstering the connection.

Compromise – the equalizer

In the face of conflict, the equalizer finds middle ground, trade-offs, and exchanges. People who look towards compromise often believe that everyone must give a little to get what they want or to resolve a conflict. Equalizers attempt to meet as many of their own goals as possible without seriously harming the relationship. Compromise involves each side giving up something in order to gain a part of what is most wanted. As an extra bonus, seeking an even split between positions often results in a quick resolution.

Compromising is a good strategy to use when:

> ➤ You want to find a quick balance between meeting goals and building or maintaining a relationship

> ➤ Time and resources are limited

> ➤ You are under pressure to reach an agreement

> ➤ The relationship is more important than the outcome

Compromise can be carried too far. Settling on a quick compromise may mean that a better solution remains hidden. Before you jump into a compromise, ask the other side, "How can I make it right?" You may be surprised to learn that the other side wants less than you expect, making a real win-win situation easier to come by.

Collaborate – the problem solver

In the face of conflict, the problem solver questions, analyzes, and collaborates. Unlike the other four approaches, collaborating problem solvers work towards achieving personal goals as well as improving relationships. People who use this strategy focus on confronting the problem, not the other party. So, they seek ways to integrate their interests with the interests of the person on the other side. Collaborators are often seen in a positive light, and the people in their inner circles generally enjoy living, working, and doing business with them. However, while this may sound like the ideal strategy, it's not appropriate for every situation. Collaboration can be time consuming and often requires a commitment to the process that is not realistic unless a high level of connection already exists.

Collaborating is a good strategy to use when:

> The issues and relationships involved are very important

> It is critical to meet goals and improve/maintain the relationship

> You can dedicate the necessary time and resources to the process

> The people around the table are committed to one another

> A significant level of trust between the parties exists or can be built

> You are all prepared to confront the problem, not each other

> Your goal is to create a solution that satisfies everyone involved

> You want to promote a positive cycle of interaction and avoid the negative cycle of bad feelings generated by a get-even seesaw

> Merging different perspectives will prove beneficial

> Everyone involved is able to remain undogmatic and flexible

> Those who will carry out the solution are committed to it

> The objective is to learn, test assumptions, and understand another's views

> You want or need a thorough exploration of the issues

When you're considering problem-solving collaboration as a strategy, ask yourself these questions:

> Are the time and resources that are necessary to engage in this process available?

> Will setting a positive tone and having a flexible dialogue help me end or avoid a cycle of bad feelings?

> Is my objective to learn, test assumptions, or understand someone else's views?

> Are the issues and relationships involved very important to me?

> Can I secure a firm commitment to work together from the people on the other side?

If you can answer yes to these questions, problem-solving collaboration will usually be your best option for success.

Make a note

Only compromising and collaborating provide both a benefit to the relationship and a focus on attaining an individual goal. However, when we are emotionally triggered, it is often difficult to compromise or collaborate. Instead, we snap into the fight-or-flight mode, and we combat, avoid, or accommodate. Next time, before you allow your reaction to drive your action, count to 10. Then, consider your response and allow yourself to consciously choose from among all five styles—picking the one with the greatest potential for effective conflict management.

The conflict-management gamut – methods for managing conflict

People in conflict can use a wide variety of methods to resolve or manage their conflicts. In a perfect world, you wouldn't need all these methods. Instead, every time you found yourself in conflict, you would be able to sit down with the person on the other side and hash out your differences. However, as you have already learned, when we perceive a threat and start responding from the reptile brain, effective negotiation and discussion becomes difficult. So, other methods are necessary.

In this section, you will learn about seven conflict-management methods:

➤ Insight

➤ Negotiation

➤ Facilitation

➤ Mediation

➤ Arbitration

➤ Litigation

➤ Unilateral power

These methods can be plotted along a **Conflict Management Continuum.**

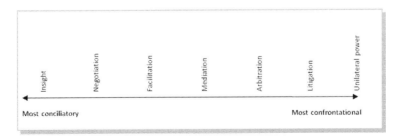

At one end of the continuum is **insight** (or **conscious conflict ownership**). At the other end is **unilateral power**. In the middle, the possibilities are just about endless.

Conscious Conflict Ownership

Conscious conflict ownership is *self-reflection* that is used to provide insight into a bigger picture. This process involves your ability to reflect on your own behavior in order to assess your real or perceived contribution to a conflict, along with the willingness to accept responsibility for that contribution. Your conscious conflict ownership functions like a mirror helping you see your blind spots and unconscious patterns. This reflection allows you to gauge your position and posture, and adjust and improve your standing. In *Chapter 5, Becoming an Expert Conflict Manager – Self-reflection and Skill Development*, I discuss conflict conscious ownership and the ways you can use this process in greater detail.

Negotiation

Negotiation is a component of almost every human interaction. We negotiate nearly all of life's transactions and conflicts. The process of negotiation involves two or more people in conversation, working together to bridge their individual agendas and reach a mutually acceptable resolution. Some people are born negotiators. Others have to learn the basics and practice in order to become effective. In *Chapter 5, Becoming an Expert Conflict Manager – Self-reflection and Skill Development*, I will present you with a crash course in negotiation so that you can move towards mastering this critical skill.

Action Point

In the meantime, as you go about your daily interactions, observe yourself and your negotiations. You are already familiar with the five basic negotiation styles—avoid, accommodate, compromise, combat, and collaborate. Today, see if you can catch yourself using all of these styles.

Facilitation

Facilitation is an experiential process that can be used for the following:

> Problem-solving

> Teaching content

> Providing structure

> Conflict management

> Tapping into the wisdom of a group or team

> Gathering or sharing information

> Creating a collaborative work environment

> Team building

> ➤ Strategic planning
> ➤ Goal setting
> ➤ Debriefing
> ➤ Group decision making

Typically, the facilitator designs an interactive process and then acts as a guide as the group members move through a set of activities. The process is frequently used at corporate retreats and other events where a group of stakeholders needs to work collectively. You can learn more about facilitation from the International Association of Facilitators (www.iaf-world.org).

Mediation

When communication is difficult or derailed, an impartial mediator can provide a forum for dialogue. The mediator acts as the guardian of the process, while the parties control what is discussed as well as the outcome. A skilled mediator helps the people in conflict move their blinders back so that their focal points can shift away from their positions and their projections of possible legal outcomes toward their **interests** (see the Lemon story on the next page, for an example and an explanation of the concept of interests).

Arbitration

Arbitration is sometimes considered litigation lite. This process employs a decision-making arbitrator who, like a judge, decides how the parties' dispute will be resolved based on the arbitrator's interpretation of legal rights and industry standards. Arbitration differs from litigation in that (a) arbitration may be binding or nonbinding, (b) the rules of evidence are relaxed, and (c) arbitration does not typically provide an option to subsequently appeal the arbitrator's decision.

Litigation

Litigation involves the use of a lawsuit to obtain an outcome that is based on legal rights. The process typically involves a series of steps that may lead to a court trial where the parties involved present their cases to a judge, who decides the outcome based on his/her interpretation of the law.

Unilateral power

Unilateral power is commonly used by dictators and gangster bosses. Those who wield this form of power ultimately have the ability to directly or indirectly influence others in a coercive or persuasive way. These power brokers decide outcomes without regard to the law or fair treatment of the people involved. Violence, intimidation, and fear are typically used to make unilateral power work.

The Lemon story

Before we go any further, it's time to explain the concept of *interests*, which was mentioned earlier in the *Mediation* section. The best way to illustrate this point is to tell you the story of the Lemon sisters, three sisters who were fighting over a lemon. Each sister had the same position: "I want the lemon. The lemon belongs to me."

The sisters didn't understand each other's perspectives. Instead, each sister blamed the other two for their problems. None of the sisters possessed enough *conscious conflict ownership* to be able to look at the dispute through a lens that allowed her to see the interplay between their individual thoughts, feelings, and actions.

The sisters did try to *negotiate*. However, their efforts were unsuccessful. Each one allowed emotional triggers from the past to block her ability to share stories in a way that made them easy to hear. The sisters did not listen to one another with curiosity and compassion. Their dysfunctional communication patterns didn't foster mutual understanding or act as a bridge to finding solutions.

The sisters considered hiring an impartial *facilitator* who could take them through some activities and help them create a strategic plan for the lemon's future. However, the sisters were already angry at one another, and they didn't want to work together

Arbitration was suggested. They did seek out a lemon arbitrator who would make a decision based on the law and the lemon industry standards. However, each sister was concerned that she might lose and would have to walk out of the hearing with her tail between her legs (metaphorically, of course). So, no arbitrator was hired.

Each sister consulted a lawyer, separately, and discussed the possibility of *litigation*. The lawyers explained that if they took their dispute to court, each of them would then have to attempt to prove that she was the one who had a legal right to the lemon. The sisters learned that they would have to bring in expensive lemon DNA experts, witnesses, and documents. All of this evidence would be offered as proof of the lemon's legal ownership and, ultimately, a judge would determine the lemon's legitimate owner. Someone would be the clear winner, and someone else would be the clear loser. Ultimately, though, even the winner would lose as the relationship with her sisters would have significantly deteriorated as a result of the adversarial nature of the litigation processes.

Ultimately, the sisters knew they couldn't spend their time or money on court procedures. Their Aunt Tilly, the family matriarch, told them that they should just cut the lemon in thirds. This way, each of them would get a fraction of what she wanted without further damaging their relationship. Tilly told them that she was so sick of hearing about the lemon that she would kill all of them if they didn't stop fighting (and the sisters feared that Tilly just might do it).

So, out of fear, the sisters were ready to cut the lemon in thirds, when they happened to meet a mediator. As the story goes (and remember, I am a mediator and this is a mediator's story), the sisters then began a collaborative dialogue with their skilled mediator (that's all mediation is—collaborative dialogue, an assisted conversation). Through the mediator's thought-provoking questions and their ensuing conversation, the sisters were able to put their positions ("I want the lemon") aside and focused instead on uncovering their *interests*. That's when it became apparent that Zelda, the eldest sister, wanted the lemon so that she could grate the rind, get the zest, and make a lemon cake. Mabel, the middle sister, wanted the lemon juice so that she could make lemonade, and Phoebe, the youngest sister, wanted the lemon seeds so that she could plant them and grow more lemons. Their *interests* are the rind, the juice, and the seeds. Their possibilities for ongoing lemon projects are enormous.

Make a note

In the real world, it's often not easy to uncover interests. However, when people in conflict sit together and converse, the possibility greatly increases. Sorting out interests is the first step to coming up with creative win-win resolutions.

If you are able to focus on interests, not positions, you may never need a mediator. Instead, you can use interest-based negotiation, a concept that comes out of the Program on Negotiation at Harvard. Interest-based negotiators focus on relationship building, mutual benefit, and working together to solve the problem versus trying to annihilate the person on the other side.

Make a note

A conflict coach works one on one with clients who are experiencing a conflict with another person. Typically, the coach and the client will talk about the client's conflict, consider options to manage the conflict, and design an approach to handle the conflict. Conflict coaching can be useful in a variety of situations, including workplace conflicts, divorce, community disputes, family disagreements, or business conflicts. The conflict coach serves as a confidential listener and sounding board who helps the client see the situation from a different perspective, consider other options, create a plan of action to deal with the conflict, and rehearse the conversation that will ultimately take place with the person on the other side.

Self-assessment

When you have time to sit and reflect, answer the following questions:

➤ Which of the five negotiation or conflict-management styles do you naturally prefer?

➤ Do you stretch and use other styles, or do you almost always respond to conflict using the style you're most comfortable with?

➤ Think about the last conflict you encountered:

  ➢ Which conflict-management style did you use?

  ➢ Was this the best choice?

  ➢ Could another approach have produced better results?

Further reading

You can find various quizzes and surveys that will help you determine your preferred conflict-management or conflict-negotiation style. Take a look at these:

➤ http://www.ncsu.edu/grad/preparing-future-leaders/docs/conflict-management-styles-quiz.pdf

➤ http://academic.engr.arizona.edu/vjohnson/ConflictManagementQuestionnaire/ConflictManagementQuestionnaire.asp

➤ http://www.agrisk.umn.edu/conference/uploads/CTerhune0790_02.pdf

➤ http://www.elcamino.edu/faculty/bcarr/documents/ConflictManagementStyle.pdf

Action Point

Consider using these assessment tools with your colleagues at work in order to open up a dialogue about conflict management.

Summary

No one conflict-management style or method will fit every conflict. Instead, effective conflict managers consider and evaluate how to best serve the parties involved and help them reach a desired outcome. In deciding which process to use, the parties and their advisors should consider their goals, motives, and needs; any current or on-going relationships; financial and time constraints; the need for privacy; the predictability of the legal outcome; and the existing power imbalances. You are now equipped to select both the best individual strategy and the best method or process to handle a specific conflict, because in this chapter, you learned:

- When to use each of the five conflict-management styles:
    - Avoid
    - Accommodate
    - Combat
    - Compromise
    - Collaborate

- How seven conflict-management methods work and when each of them is the best choice:
    - Insight
    - Negotiation
    - Facilitation
    - Mediation
    - Arbitration
    - Litigation
    - Unilateral power

In the next chapter, you will learn more about conscious conflict ownership, negotiation, and listening. That chapter is about skill development. When you are done, you will be much better equipped to handle the conflicts around you, both at home and at work.

> 5

Becoming an Expert Conflict Manager – Self-reflection and Skill Development

This book is designed to build on your natural attributes and talents and the skills and knowledge you have acquired and developed through other life experiences. Having read this far, you are already knowledgeable about conflict dynamics, aware of the styles individuals use to manage conflicts, and acquainted with the key methods that can be used to resolve or manage conflicts.

This chapter will take you to the next level and enable you to sharpen three key skills: conscious conflict ownership, negotiation, and listening. These are critical as you become an expert in conflict prevention and conflict management. At the end of this chapter, you will understand:

> ➤ The conscious conflict ownership mindset and four things you can do to achieve it

> ➤ The negotiation process and how you can prepare yourself for masterful negotiations

> ➤ Effective listening strategies and how you can use them in your conflict-management toolbox

Awakening your conscious conflict ownership

Our conflicts are our best teachers. Few of us grow, change, or learn in the absence of conflict. **Conscious conflict ownership** is the ability to look at your conflicts and clearly see how you created or co-created the situation, where you are, and where you could be. Like a mirror, conscious conflict ownership, helps you see your blind spots and unconscious patterns. This reflection allows you to gauge your position and posture, and adjust and improve your standing.

> *"We don't see things as they are, we see them as we are."* - Anais Nin

Conscious conflict ownership is about accessing information at a deeper level. This information can bring you a sense of connectedness as well as an inner knowing that allows you to see beyond your blind spots. Today, the concept of conscious awareness is being embraced as a powerful tool to transcend unconscious patterns. Even people who would have previously dismissed the idea as flakey are now open to becoming acquainted with what is going on at deeper levels.

Conscious conflict ownership is conscious awareness that enables you to look at your conflicts through a sharper lens so that you can see how your decisions and actions interact with other factors and forces. It is about seeing the previously unseen and recognizing how your thoughts, feelings, and actions impact others. Conscious conflict ownership enables you to see your own conflicts from different perspectives, grasp the lessons these conflicts can provide, and incorporate those lessons into your life.

When we are involved in conflict, sometimes, it is possible to unravel and sort through the conflict on our own. In fact, the person on the other side may never even have to know that the conflict exists. Conscious conflict ownership occurs when you are able to look at an existing conflict, see your contribution to it, and change your position, attitude, actions, or reactions. When you find that a conflict has gone away entirely, seemingly on its own, you have probably experienced conscious conflict ownership.

The components of conscious conflict ownership

There are four main components to conscious conflict ownership, as follows:

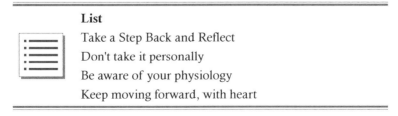

List

Take a Step Back and Reflect

Don't take it personally

Be aware of your physiology

Keep moving forward, with heart

Now, let's understand each one.

Take a step back and reflect

When you step back from conflict you can see the bigger picture and reflect upon your part in its creation. Doing this will help you develop your insight and critical thinking and increase your willingness to be accountable for your own actions and reactions, rather than blaming others.

Don't take it personally

In *The Four Agreements: A Practical Guide to Personal Freedom*, Don Miguel Ruiz, a leader in the conscious awareness community, tells us:

> *"Don't take it personally. Nothing others do is because of you. What others say and do is a projection of their own reality, their own dream. When you are immune to the opinions and actions of others, you won't be the victim of needless suffering."*

It's easy to fall into the take-it-personally trap. In reality, other people are acting and reacting based on what is best for them. Everyone is focused on their own little world. When we are able to accept things as they are and recognize that when someone else's actions irritate, hurt, or annoy us, it's not about us, but about them; the benefit is a sense of freedom.

Be aware of your physiology

Physical sensations and emotions provide important messages. But we have been programmed to ignore them. The subtle rumblings of feeling dismissed, discounted, disrespected, disenfranchised, or otherwise devalued can build-up to the point of no return. However, when you address these sensations, which are actually part of the fight or flight survival response in your nervous system, before you are propelled into explosion, you can avoid conflict drama and come out the winner.

Keep moving forward, with heart

Acknowledge your mistakes, make positive suggestions for the future, follow up when appropriate, and ultimately learn from (and avoid repeating) your missteps. When you engage in this forward motion, without harsh self-talk, you will find yourself open to the lessons that your conflicts can provide.

Accessing conscious conflict ownership

Yes, aligning your mindset to embrace Conscious Conflict Ownership is no small task. But, it's worth the work. When you are able to look at an existing conflict, see your individual contributions to it, and change your position, attitude, actions, or reactions, you may find that the conflict has gone away entirely, seemingly on its own. Ultimately, Conscious Conflict Ownership will bring you pay-offs that include improved relationships, a reduction in the amount and intensity of your conflicts, and a better understanding of yourself and your world.

Action Point

When you have time and space, write down or otherwise recount the story of a significant conflict you faced from the perspective of the person on the other side. Think of this as a role-play exercise; you are an actor, playing a role. Imagine what this person might say about what they saw, heard, or felt. Consider all the factors that this person lives with. Describe how the stressors of their life might have impacted them. Think of ways in which they could justify their actions based on their circumstances.

Next, figure out what the two of you have in common. Is there any place that your goals complement one another? For instance, in the workplace, you may both be perceived as childish or catty if you continue to fight. If you can put your differences behind you, both of your reputations will benefit. Knowing that you both want the same thing—for instance, to look good to the boss—doesn't mean it's an either/or. You can both accomplish this goal. Conscious conflict ownership involves the willingness to see options that have been beyond your vision until now. Believing there is enough to go around will enable you to stop fighting for crumbs.

The benefits of conscious conflict ownership

When your mindset is aligned with conscious conflict ownership, the payoffs include increased trust, a bridging of the gaps between different perspectives and cultures, engaged stakeholders, and sustained collaboration, all of which are increasingly important in business.

Make a note

On a personal, tribal, or global level (think of your workplace as a tribe), conscious conflict ownership enables you to better understand yourself and your world.

Becoming a master negotiator

We are all negotiating all the time. The baby crying for his bottle is negotiating. The diplomat involved in an international dispute is negotiating. The mother and teenager who are trying to find a mutually acceptable curfew are negotiating.

Negotiation is a process of direct discussion. We negotiate transactions and conflicts, everything from which restaurant we'll choose for lunch to how to structure our businesses and our lives. Almost everything, in every aspect of your life, is negotiable. Effective negotiation skills are one critical key to achieving success. Especially in these difficult economic times, your ability to negotiate may mean the difference between achievement and failure.

Make a note

One of the important components of an effective negotiation is having negotiators who are willing to become partners and patiently seek out creative resolutions. This doesn't necessarily mean splitting the difference. Instead, masterful negotiation often involves sharing stories in a way that makes them easy to hear, as well as listening with curiosity and compassion. Such open communication fosters mutual understanding and acts like a bridge to finding solutions.

The negotiation process

The negotiation process itself is fluid or circular, moving through five phases:

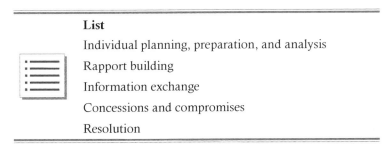

List

Individual planning, preparation, and analysis

Rapport building

Information exchange

Concessions and compromises

Resolution

Individual planning, preparation, and analysis

In the information age, each of us has quick and easy access to information. Do your homework! If you are going to make an offer on a house, you should know how much every comparable house sold for in the last year. If you are going to apply for a job, you should learn about the company before you send your resume. Critical information is available online. So, before you ever meet the person on the other side, prepare. Find out as much as you can about your fellow negotiator and what their interests might be. Learn the facts and know your alternatives.

Rapport building

When you are able to build a rapport with the person on the other side, trust and commitment come along as part of the package. Find out about the people on the other side. Get to know them.

Information exchange

During this part of the process, information about the product or service is disclosed and the first offer is conveyed.

Concessions and compromises

Using a variety of persuasive techniques, each party focuses on priorities and tradeoffs.

Resolution

When there are multiple issues, the process circles back through each phase again.

Mastering the negotiation process

Some people are born negotiators. Others have to learn the basics and practice to become effective.

Action Point

As you go about your daily interactions, observe yourself and your negotiations. Can you find yourself moving through the five phases? In which phase are you most comfortable? In which phase do you feel the most uncomfortable or challenged?

In the meantime, follow these tips to ensure that you handle each stage of the negotiation process like a pro.

Attitude is everything

Instead of seeing your negotiations as stressful hurdles, approach every negotiation as an opportunity to explore meaningful and positive possibilities.

Be ready to hear things that you don't like

Keep in mind that when the person on the other side points out weaknesses in your position, this is part of the process. They are flexing their persuasive muscle. Don't become defensive or reactive. Instead, seek out ways to equalize strengths and weaknesses as you focus on moving forward.

Do your homework

When it comes to real estate, it's often said that the three most important factors are location, location, and location. When it comes to negotiation, the three most important factors are preparation, preparation, and preparation. How do you prepare? Do your homework so that you are clear about the following:

> ➤ The facts

> ➤ Your best option, in case you choose not to accept the deal that is being presented

> ➤ The other side and what their interests might be (remember the Lemon sisters' story and focus on interests, not positions)

Work with the other side, not against them

Use your best communication skills:

> ➤ Be clear and concise

> ➤ Ask open-ended questions

> ➤ Remain flexible and open to unseen possibilities

> ➤ Be quiet and listen

Seek to understand the cultural and personality factors that may impact the process

Remember, culture is more than one's ethnic background. Cultures and subcultures have their own sets of values and norms. In order to understand a cultural influence, you first have to *know* what culture someone identifies with. Often, this is not easy. Cultural identity is influenced by a variety of factors including religion, ancestry, skin color, language, socioeconomic status, education, profession, family connections, and political attitudes. Some people use their clothing, jewelry, tattoos, and other symbols to make a statement about which cultural groups they identify with. However, much of the time, there is no recognizable expression. While some people are delighted to discuss their cultural identity and will welcome your questions, others will be offended. In order to avoid an uncomfortable situation, always invest time in *observing* before you make assumptions.

Be prepared for dirty negotiation tactics

Dirty tactics tend to fall into three categories:

➤ **Deliberate deception**. This takes the form of lies, exaggeration, and omission regarding the facts at hand, willingness or ability to settle, or the bottom line

➤ **Psychological manipulation**. This typically plays out with an attempt to either garner sympathy or intimidate, with histrionics, bullying, good guy/bad guy, personal attacks, or threats

➤ **Positional pressure tactics**. This involves taking a hardline position and refusing to negotiate, making extreme demands, offering a take-it-or-leave-it ultimatum, or upping the demands after an offer has been accepted

When faced with a dirty negotiator, you have the following three options:

➤ Identify and confront the dirty tactic

➤ Fall prey to it, because you are desperate

➤ Walk away

Make your decision based on the circumstances and your motivation. Remember, you choose your response.

Learning to listen

Make a note

Listening is one of the most powerful tools in your conflict-management toolbox.

People tend to close down and stay stuck in their positions until they feel heard. So, trying to engage in problem solving before everyone feels heard can be like trying to paint on a canvas that is already covered with gobs of paint. In fact, sometimes, all it takes to defuse a conflict is to allow everyone involved time to vent.

The dictionary defines listening as "making an effort to hear something," or "paying attention." The listener "concentrates on hearing something and pays attention." The simple act of listening can be difficult, especially for those of us who like to talk or feel we have something to add to the conversation.

We have two ears, but only one mouth. Need I say more? In order to get the whole story, you have to shut up and listen. Being quiet is the first step, but it's not enough when you want someone else to know that you are really listening. As most of us receive no training in good listening, here is your crash course. When you are done, go out and practice your listening skills. Practice will make progress.

The five levels of listening

Communication experts have identified these five levels of listening:

> ➤ **Ignoring** is the opposite of listening. Ignoring is an active choice not to pay attention to someone or something.

> ➤ **Pretending** is what happens when our minds are elsewhere, but we want to give the speaker the impression that we are listening.

> ➤ **Selective listening** is about paying attention to bits and pieces of information. In this mixture of hearing and listening, we select portions to listen to and pretend or ignore the rest.

> ➤ **Active listening** is an active engagement in the communication process. When we are actively listening, we help the listening process along ourselves.

> ➤ **Attentive listening** is a subtle and powerful style of listening. The attentive listener is engaged with the speaker, but this engagement is more about presence than active involvement. The attentive listener pays attention to the speaker's words and focuses energy on his messages. Others know when we are attentively listening; they see it reflected in our physical and emotional responses.

Make a note

Both active and attentive listening require an open, unbiased, and uncluttered mind.

Becoming an active listener

Many of the following active-listening techniques do not come naturally, so please practice them everywhere you can:

List

Position yourself either face to face or shoulder to shoulder ("Let's go for a walk") with the speaker.

Make effective and appropriate **eye contact**. You should mimic the eye contact that each party seems comfortable with.

Make appropriate **facial gestures.**

Give affirmative **head nods**. Remember, however, that nodding can be interpreted as agreement as opposed to understanding, so be clear what the nod means.

Be **present**. Pay strict attention to all speakers and avoid actions or gestures that suggest boredom, such as yawning or leaning on your hand.

Ask. Use two types of question: open-ended (how, what, when, where, who) to gather information and clarifying questions to check understanding.

Paraphrase. Use your own (neutral) words to let the speaker know that they have been heard.

Repeat the exact words that someone has said. This can be especially helpful when the speaker is in a lot of emotional pain or when you disagree with them completely.

Reframe. Take a part of what the speaker has said and focus in on it. This way, you can amplify something the person has said that you want to focus on while other content falls outside the frame.

Summarize. "In a nutshell……"

Empathize. Acknowledge and validate the feelings and thoughts behind the words ("I can understand why you felt betrayed").

Prompt. If there is a significant break in the conversation, use one or two words to encourage the speaker to continue.

Pick up on **nonverbal clues**. Just make sure that you check out your assumptions ("I sense a lot of sadness, is that correct?").

Don't interrupt the speaker and don't talk too much.

The best listeners

Effective listeners know that the goal is to *understand the message, not judge it*. They do this by listening for data that disproves rather than supports their beliefs. This means resisting the natural urge to defend, correct, disprove, or question what the other person is saying.

Finally, remember that when a party in conflict is sharing their perceptions, it usually doesn't matter if the perception is accurate or not. It doesn't matter if the perception is in alignment with your beliefs. All that matters is that this is the way the speaker sees it.

Self-assessment

When you have time to sit and reflect, answer the following questions:

List

What are your three greatest strengths?

What are your three greatest weaknesses?

Do you see any overlap between your greatest strengths and greatest weaknesses?

Often, strengths and weaknesses are two sides of the same coin. In fact, most traits can present as either an asset or a liability, depending on the situation and the observer. For example, if you are wise and intuitive, you might also come across as a know-it-all. If you are gentle and kind, you could also be seen as weak.

We can use our traits to soothe conflicts or inflame them. How can you best use your strengths and weaknesses so that you are viewed as a skilled conflict manager?

Further reading

There is always more to learn about negotiation. In order to keep learning, take a look at the following resources:

➤ Cohen, H. (2006). *Negotiate This!: By Caring, But Not That Much, Business Plus.*

➤ Diamond, S. (2010). *Getting more: How to negotiate to achieve your goals in the real world, Random House/Crown Business.*

➤ Fisher, R. & Ury, W. (1991). *Getting to yes: Negotiating agreement without giving in, Penguin.*

➤ Mnookin, R.H., Peppet, S.R., Tulumello, A.S. (2004). *Beyond winning: Negotiating to create value in deals and disputes, Belknap Press of Harvard University Press.*

➤ Shell, G.R. (2006). *Bargaining for advantage: Negotiation strategies for reasonable people (2nd Ed.), Penguin.*

Summary

This chapter was about skill development. In this chapter, you learned that:

> ➤ You can achieve conscious conflict ownership

> ➤ You are prepared for masterful negotiations

> ➤ You can use listening strategies to diffuse the conflicts you encounter

In the next chapter, you will learn about conflict conversations, including how to hold a difficult discussion, how to analyze a conflict and define the real issue, how to fight smart and fight fair, and how to make magical apologies.

> 6

Conflict Conversations

Frequently, the only two options we see to handle an uncomfortable situation are to respond in a combative manner (fight) or totally avoid the issues (flight). Sadly, both of these strategies often do more to escalate our misery than to extinguish it. On the other hand, when we are able to use conversation to clear the air, we can create a sense of connection and dedication to starting over with a clean slate. Before you can get that breath of fresh air, however, a very uncomfortable conversation may need to take place. In this chapter, you will learn how to hold these difficult conversations.

After you read this chapter, you will be more confident when it's time to hold an uncomfortable conversation. You will know:

- ➤ How to hold a difficult discussion
- ➤ How to analyze and define an issue that is fueling a workplace conflict
- ➤ How to fight smart and fight fair
- ➤ How to make a magical apology
- ➤ How to deal with difficult people

Difficult discussions

Whether your difficult discussion involves a confrontation or bringing up a topic that makes everyone squirm, this section gives you a model to hold your talk. Before we get to the nuts and bolts, there are three things you should know about holding difficult discussions.

Make a note

Confrontation, venting, and strong emotions are often part of the process. Knowing up front that this conversation may not be pretty will help you keep your cool and model the attitudes and behaviors you want from others.

Focusing on solving problems is more effective than placing blame. Fault finding is looking backward; resolution requires moving forward.

Your tone of voice and body language should be in agreement with your words. Others will believe your tone and other nonverbal messages rather than your words if there is inconsistency between them.

Ten steps for difficult discussions

The good news is that you can sort out even the nastiest subjects if both of you are willing to come to the table and remain committed to building the relationship. Here is my 10-step plan to holding difficult discussions.

Step 1 – prepare

Make some notes about the situation and your feelings. Write about where you are, where you want to be, and how you might get there. Consider the best, worst, and probable outcome to your circumstances. Finally, before you hold a difficult discussion, you should ask yourself the following 12 questions:

Are you willing to risk damaging or losing the relationship? If not, you may not want to engage in this conversation. You cannot put the toothpaste back in the tube, and you cannot take back your words once you have shared them with someone else.

Is this a relationship that you want or need to save? If not, you may not want to engage in the discussion. It may be better to just move on.

Are you going to ask the person on the other side to change? If you are, you may want to think twice. It's difficult to change even when we are highly motivated. It's almost impossible to change when the stimulus for change is coming from an external force.

What is the best location to hold the discussion? Is a comfortable, neutral meeting location available?

What political forces are sustaining the conflict? Who needs to be involved in the discussion? And, who needs to be involved in the implementation of any possible resolutions?

What are the possible consequences of admitting a mistake, losing emotional control, or exposing a personal vulnerability?

What level of confidentiality is reasonable to expect?

Should any topics or solutions be off limits?

How can the situation be framed as a mutual problem?

Should there be any guidelines or ground rules? Personally, I am not a fan of guidelines. Some people will rebel at the mere mention of the word. Typically, business meetings do not need guidelines; we just assume that everyone will act in a reasonable and mature manner. However, if you believe that you need to lay out some guidelines before beginning your difficult discussion, make sure you avoid framing them in the negative (no name calling). Instead, stay positive (a commitment to show each other respect).

How long should this discussion be? Do you want to set a time limit or just let things flow? Setting a time limit provides structure and a way out. Leaving things open-ended, however, often allows for a critical unfolding of thoughts and feelings. There is no one-size-fits-all format. Consider all possibilities.

Does the person on the other side know that there is a problem? Do they know that something is bothering you, or will this conversation come as a surprise?

Step 2 – call a truce

Be willing to come to the table and stay there. The other side will come if your message is "I want to find solutions that work for both of us." If you cannot carry the message, find someone who can intervene on your behalf and get you both to the table.

Step 3 – set the stage

Sit down at a time when you are both clear headed and able to give this important conversation the time and energy it deserves.

Step 4 – speak from the heart

Do not point fingers of blame. Instead, focus on finding solutions that work for both of you. This is collaboration. Make sure that your attitude reflects the fact that discord is simply a natural by-product of close human connection and almost always presents an opportunity for mutual learning. The following set of questions can be used to guide an effective discussion under stress:

List

Where are we now?

Where do we need to be?

How will we get there?

What do each of us need to do?

How can I help you?

Step 5 – listen, listen, listen

Listen as if you are an outside observer with no prior knowledge of the situation. 25 years in the mediation business has taught me that there are at least two sides to every story. You may be very surprised when you hear the rest of the story.

Step 6 – give yourselves time

Time gives you a chance to think, process new information, and cool down. If a discussion escalates so that people are no longer listening to each other, call a time-out. If stories are inconsistent, suggest wiping the slate clean, putting the incident in the past, and starting anew. If you are stuck and unable to find a solution, suggest writing down your perspectives of the dispute and some recommended remedies. Then, read each other's writings.

Step 7 – define the emotions

Under almost every human conflict, someone feels dismissed, discounted, disenfranchised, or disrespected. These are the emotions that fuel our feuds. Sometimes, just defining that emotion and realizing that everyone involved feels somehow devalued is enough to resolve the dispute.

Step 8 – be willing to apologize

The closer the relationship, the more likely you are to have stepped on each other's toes. If you cannot bring yourself to apologize for anything specific, at least apologize for the distress that the other side has been living with and anything they believe you did to contribute to it. When you are willing to apologize for your errors and the stress that the situation has caused the others involved, they will usually find it difficult to continue arguing. Additionally, the apology can serve as the pivot that gets everyone to stop looking towards the past and move instead into the solution-focused future.

Step 9 – don't leave conflicts unresolved

An agreement to disagree is resolution. On the other hand, leaving a conflict open-ended sets you up for future fights. End your conversation by shaking hands and signing off on a written version of the agreed-upon solution. Include some kind of formal or informal follow-up in the agreement in order to avoid a recurrence of the conflict. (A follow-up should be a key component of any difficult discussion.) Don't expect to find flawless solutions. A solution that can be revisited and readjusted may be a great first step.

Step 10 – if all else fails, hire a professional to help you

Often, an outside opinion sheds light on your blind spots and helps reach an agreement. Consider bringing in a mediator if you need additional help with an important relationship.

Conflict analysis and defining the real issue

As we discussed in *Chapter 1, All About Conflict*, my 25 years in the mediation business has taught me that under every human conflict, someone feels dismissed, discounted, disenfranchised, or disrespected. Sometimes, this sense of being devalued cannot be traced back. You might know that you feel it and not know where it came from. Other times, the root cause is a difference that can be easily identified.

Defining and understanding the root cause of a conflict often allows a shift away from right/wrong thinking and towards a more inclusive, bigger picture. This section will show you how to identify conflicts that are based in culture, communication, values, vision, and appreciation style differences. Once these conflicts are better defined, they can be more easily defused.

Defining differences

Each of us has personal biases, prejudices, and styles that are the product of our individual natures, personal experiences, and backgrounds. Our preferences grow out of the cultures we identify with, the interaction and communication styles we are naturally comfortable with, our values, our visions for the future, and how we show others that we appreciate them. When these differences clash, conflicts often blossom.

If you can point to (or define) a specific difference, people in conflict can sometimes see that their differences do not have to be resolved with an either/or. Instead, they can often accept that their differences may be able to exist simultaneously, and they can just move on.

When you want to analyze a conflict, it can be helpful to consider differences in:

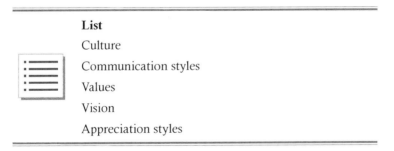

List

Culture

Communication styles

Values

Vision

Appreciation styles

Generally, once you are able to define these differences, those involved will be better able to accept them and move on.

Culture

Culture is more than nationality. No doubt you have already experienced the significant cultural differences between women and men. Likewise, millennials are culturally different from baby boomers. Often, an employee who has been indoctrinated into a corporate culture that stresses conformity to corporate policy and rules may confuse a more entrepreneurial coworker, who makes snap-decisions as she searches for innovative ideas. Members of specific cultures and subcultures have their own sets of values and norms. When people from different cultures and subcultures come together in the workplace, friction, blowups, and misunderstanding may ensue.

Culture affects the way people view and deal with conflict. Some cultures normalize high emotion, while in other cultures, people are expected to be rational and courteous even when they are embroiled in conflict. These differences may leave people feeling confused, intimidated, repulsed, or unwilling to trust the sincerity of the person on the other side.

Communication

Think back to the communication differences we discussed in *Chapter 3, Workplace Conflict in the New Normal – The Reasons and the Costs*. In David J. Ludwig's faith-based marriage-enrichment program "The Power of We," he described two communication types: pointers and painters. Pointers get to the point. Painters, on the other hand, want to paint a detail-filled picture. To the pointer, bringing up certain issues may feel like an attack. So, the pointer's natural response is to withdraw during times of conflict. Painters do not withdraw; they do the opposite, revisiting issues over and over again, overstating for effect. Clearly, when a pointer and painter work closely together, the seeds of conflict are ripe. When you understand and spot this dynamic, it becomes clear that this is a communication style difference, not the result of malicious motives.

Make a note

Keep in mind, however, that the painter-pointer classification is often not crystal clear. I've noticed that some big talkers can be painters when speaking and pointers when listening.

Values

Values are the principles and standards that guide us as we move through life. Our values direct our actions, judgments, attitudes, and decisions about what is good, bad, right, and wrong. For most of us, our values are fluid—they change as a result of the changes in society and our individual situations.

When we are able to look behind the details of a conflict story, the warring parties' underlying motivations may be similar or opposite. This motivation, which is often expressed as intentions, hopes, dreams, or commitments, usually points to their core values. It's hard to hate someone when you share and understand their motivation. When two people share values, it's almost always a unifying factor that they can call upon to guide them in their interactions and decisions.

Make a note

Organizational psychologists have concluded that when workers share values with their supervisors and organizations, there are higher levels of satisfaction and productivity. On the other hand, a lack of shared values can tear an organization, friendship, or family apart.

Vision

Think back to the visioning exercise in *Chapter 3, Workplace Conflict in the New Normal – The Reasons and the Costs*. Your vision is your plan for the future; it's what drives where you go and how you get there. A vision that is connected to a sense of purpose is the most powerful motivator—much stronger than money. Look at Martin Luther King, Mahatma Gandhi, or Nelson Mandela. Could you pay people to do that? No. When people share a common purpose, their conflicts take a back seat.

Each of us openly express some parts of our life's vision. We all keep other parts more private, acknowledging them only as dreams for the future, if at all. When people come together with different expectations for the future, they can become discouraged by the difficulty of bringing their visions into alignment and reality.

Make a note

Often, people with competing or conflicting visions perceive the other as a threat to survival. This threat triggers the **fight-or-flight** response in the **reptilian brain** as discussed in *Chapter 1, All About Conflict*.

You may have to dig, but when you can find and define common aspects within peoples' visions, it becomes easier to move them towards unity and away from disharmony. Even the hint of a shared vision can get disputing parties back into more conscious thinking, which happens in the cerebral cortex of the brain. With a shared vision, the potential for the creation of a grander picture of the future exists. At the very least, a path to move on without stepping on one another's toes can emerge.

Appreciation style

In his book, *The Five Love Languages: How to Express Heartfelt Commitment to Your Mate*, Gary Chapman says that there are five styles people use to convey and receive love. Most of us will have a natural preference for one or two of the styles and not really connect to the others. Understanding these styles and how they are expressed in close relationships (not only romantic relationships) can help you define a conflict's root cause. We already know that conflict is often a response to one's sense of being devalued. When two people who work together face persistent conflicts, it may be because they are failing to convey or translate a sense of value or appreciation to one another.

Using Chapman's ideas, we can understand how messages of appreciation can become lost in translation when two people use different styles to express that appreciation. Chapman identifies these five languages:

> *Words of affirmation.* People who prefer this style show others appreciation with unsolicited compliments and praise. Likewise, hearing these words of affirmation from others will speak loudly, making their hearts sing.

> *Quality time.* People who prefer this style show appreciation with shared time and availability for connection and memory building. On the flip side, they will become angry and insulted when someone is distracted or misses appointments.

> *Gifts.* As Chapman explains it, this is not about materialism. Instead, for those who prefer this style, the thought and effort put into selecting and giving the gift are what shows that the giver understands and values the receiver. Likewise, a missed birthday, anniversary, or a hasty, thoughtless gift can spell disaster.

> *Acts of service.* People who prefer this style will do their fair share of the tasks at hand and then go the extra mile. In return, they want others to show appreciation by easing the burden of their responsibilities. When this doesn't happen and they believe that someone else is lazy, breaking commitments, or making more work for them, they feel unappreciated and angry.

> *Physical touch.* Appropriate in some relationships, not appropriate in others, physical affection can convey a powerful message of comfort and soothing. Acts as small as a pat on the shoulder, a handshake, or a hug can be big to people who prefer this style. In the workplace, however, physical touch can be a time bomb. Only touch others when you are sure that it is welcome and appropriate.

Action Point

When you want to know which style will convey a message of appreciation to someone, just look at the style they use to convey appreciation to others. Most of us will "speak" in the style that we find easiest to hear. For example, If someone frequently uses words of praise, they will probably be receptive to hearing your praise for them. On the other hand, someone who never uses words of praise may find your compliments insincere.

Carole and Amy have been business partners for the last 13 years. Carole's preferred languages of appreciation are *words of affirmation* and *gifts*. She is a master at gushing, heaping compliments and gifts upon those she cares about. On the other hand, Amy is a little too caustic for compliments. She tends to talk to the broken parts, looking for improvement. She just doesn't get the whole gift scene. Amy says:

> *"I have enough junk in my garage; if I want something badly enough, I usually find a way to get it, and if someone gives me a gift, I feel the need to reciprocate. Reciprocating takes time, the one thing I don't have enough of. I love spending time with the people I care about. It doesn't matter what we do, sharing a meal or taking a walk is all it takes. The connection built in time spent makes my heart and soul sing. Likewise, acts of service speak volumes to me. I want to share what I know with those I care about. If one of them can do something for me that I would otherwise have to do for myself—from making me a cup of tea to fixing my computer—it is really, really appreciated."*

Can you see how Carole and Amy might have some issues in showing each other appreciation? Without this appreciation, little things can start to snowball. Knowing that they are drawn to different appreciation styles has helped Carole and Amy clarify their expectations and made their relationship easier.

Make a note

When we analyze a conflict by pointing out the differences in culture, communication, values, vision, and appreciation styles, people in conflict are often able to see that neither of them is right, wrong, better, or worse. They are just different. Once they accept this fact, they can usually disengage, agree to disagree, and move on.

Fight smart, fight fair

Are you uncomfortable with the idea of an angry exchange? Many women feel this way. And angry exchanges at work are often the ones we fear most. Sadly, this aversion to disagree can bring more negative consequences than the original disagreement. Failing to speak-up when someone has stepped on your toes can lead to bloody feet (metaphorically) and destructive resentments. It is possible to overcome your fear of fighting and become skilled in the art of productive disagreement. This section will teach you what you need to know in order to become confident in your ability to fight smart and fight fair.

Action Point

Before you even think about bringing up an unpleasant issue, rate it on a scale of 1 to 10. Things that don't rate as an 8, 9, or 10 are usually not worth arguing about. Instead, ask yourself: 30 minutes, 30 days, or 30 years from now, will I still care about this? If not, let it go. If you will care, you need to focus in on Who? What? and When? The next section will tell you how.

Pick your fights

This is a three-part process. First, pick who you are fighting with, then pick what you are fighting about, and finally decide when to bring it up.

Who?

Make a note

If someone is a lunatic, don't waste your time. Instead, stay as far away as possible. Minimize your dealings with crazy people. This will save you time and money. I repeat, do not argue with crazy people. Even if you win, you lose.

Before you engage in any argument, make sure you are dealing with the right person. Does this person have the authority necessary to give you what you want? Do not waste your time and energy on a substitute or stand-in. It's almost always a good idea to wait for the real decision-maker to show up before you start listing your complaints.

Getting the Who? right can be a challenge. In the workplace, an employee may turn on a supervisor who is just following orders instead of going after the boss who is setting down the rules. This is not productive. It's easy to misdirect negative feelings onto someone who is an easier mark. But choosing the right person is critical to fighting smart and fighting fair.

What?

Only argue over things that can be measured. Do not argue over values and beliefs. Yesterday, I got myself in an uproar trying to convince someone that her political beliefs are full of holes. HELLO! I should know better. Ultimately, if she feels better believing stories that seem to be designed to manipulate the masses with fear, who am I to point to the alternate reality? Values and beliefs are not negotiable. Only argue over things that can result in an action plan: you will do this, I won't do that, and so on. Leave the rest of it for the pundits.

When?

If you are sure you want to go forward, think about the consequences of bringing up the topic. Timing is critical. Ask yourself if this is the best time to make your point or if it would be better to shut up now and bring it up later. In any event, avoid arguing in public at all costs.

List

There are four simple rules for a fair fight:

- Fight in the here and now. Do not bring up things that happened in the distant past.
- Listen to each other. Do not talk over someone. Instead, take turns speaking, even if you have to use a timer to make it happen.
- Keep the focus on yourself; use "I" statements to avoid pointing the finger of blame. It's not important what percentage of fault each of you contributed to the creation of the problem.
- Avoid threats, name-calling, contempt, nagging, whining, and any other communication strategy that could be seen as manipulative.

My Fight Fundamentals:

Find commonalities. Seek out similarities. Building your discussion on a foundation of points of agreement allows you to move on with a better – more harmonious – perspective.

What's in it for them? Instead of focusing on what you want, focus on what features and benefits the other person will receive. This is somewhat of a paradox but it is truly easier to get what you want when the person on the other side sees that you are trying to satisfy her also

Look at the big picture. Once you have outlined the big picture perspective you can focus in on the details.

Clearly state what you want or need. Move beyond the story and the past. Instead, create an outline of what you want and why. Once you have outlined your priorities and goals, it is easier to be future focused. We cannot negotiate what happened in the past, it's done. But, we can negotiate the future.

Stick to the facts. Your opinions and beliefs can muddy the waters. Facts are facts.

Give everyone time to think, process the information, and cool down. Everything looks different in the morning.

Speak in a language the other person understands. Don't talk feelings to your accountant. (Unless your accountant likes to talk about feelings.) This is not an excuse to be condescending or inauthentic. If you are not genuine you will come across as untrustworthy. So, seek out a balance between your state of mind and theirs.

Get positive closure. Each argument ends with one of three possible outcomes:

- ➤ Agreement
- ➤ Agree to disagree and move on
- ➤ No agreement and horns still locked

The final outcome is the resolution you don't want. Of course, just because you're here now doesn't mean this is where you'll stay. Remember, there is a HUGE difference between going away unhappy and going away so angry that getting a gun sounds like a good idea. If you "win" and the other side goes home and gets his gun, you lost.

Finally, be comfortable apologizing. A genuine apology can bring about profound change and healing. It is one way to give the "loser" an opportunity to save face. Often, you can come out the big winner when you apologize. We will discuss apologies in the next section.

Magical apologies

When you know how to craft a powerfully effective apology, you can cover your tracks without leaving blood on your hands or appearing weak. This is a must-have skill for every woman in business.

The power of the apology

As a professional mediator, I have seen the power of the apology first hand. The 12-Steps of Alcoholics Anonymous promotes the spiritual directive to "make a list of all persons we have harmed, become willing to make amends to them all, and make direct amends wherever possible" (http://12step.org/). This may be one of the best life practices you can incorporate. In fact, adopting this philosophy can drastically improve your relationships.

A genuine apology can be very powerful and go a long way towards repairing a relationship. Even if you don't want reconciliation, an apology can bring closure and internal peace as well as reduce the possibility of negative repercussions in the future. In fact, *many of the workplace disputes that end up in court could have been settled by someone making a sincere and timely apology* before things got out of control. The problem is, usually, both people think that they have been wronged. It is usually difficult to make an apology if you think that the apology should be made to you instead.

Make a note

To avoid the "I will not apologize when I did nothing wrong" trap, base your actions on the big picture. Refocus so that you can see your disputes from the vantage point of the person on the other side.

Make a note

People in the wrong are often afraid to apologize. This apology aversion is usually motivated by a belief that an apology will make them legally liable or open them up to blame and shame. However, we know that doctors who apologize to their patients for medical mistakes don't get sued nearly as much as the ones who take a more arrogant attitude. It is possible to apologize without admitting wrong doing. And, people on the receiving end of the apology are often so grateful for the apology that almost anything works.

Crafting your apology

List

When you don't want to admit wrong doing, You can simply apologize for the distress that the situation has caused both of you and your contribution to creating this distress.

When appropriate, you may want to say "I made a mistake and I am sorry. While I know we will both make mistakes in the future, hopefully, I will not repeat this mistake."

Even "I am so sorry that this is where we ended up," which allows the apologizer to escape any admission of wrong doing, when said with an earnest tone, can do wonders.

If you want to avoid rehashing the whole situation, it's okay to let the receiver know that it is not your intention to discuss the situation—you just want to apologize.

What makes a sincere apology?

A sincere apology is one that is made with no expectations for how the other side will respond.

There are three possible responses to any apology. They are as follows:

> The receiver accepts the apology, and the parties go forward with the goal of re-establishing their connection

> The receiver accepts the apology, and the parties agree to disagree and move on—with their connection severed

> The party that is receiving the apology is unable to accept it

Even with this last response, the giver of the apology can feel that she has done her part and kept her side of the street clean. Sometimes, even the most heartfelt apology is not enough to re-establish a connection. People come into our lives for a reason, a season, or a lifetime. When it comes to workplace relationships, it is often not clear, especially initially, how long someone will be around.

An apology can be magical, cleansing, and healing. Who do you need to apologize to?

Dealing with difficult people

Sadly, each of us will periodically encounter people who are unreasonable and difficult. This section will teach you strategies to use to effectively deal with these miserable characters.

Some people are overly sensitive, discerning, suspicious, insecure, or needy. However, if you treat them right, many of these people can become assets within your inner circle. These people may have had negative experiences in the past that have compromised their abilities to trust and connect. However, they can be turned around if they understand that you value and accept them. Ultimately you may be able to turn some of these difficult people into intensely loyal friends and allies.

On the other hand, the truly difficult person will delight in keeping you off balance by acting up. These difficult people appear immune to good manners, honest communication, and caring. In general, difficult people fall into six categories, with some difficult people exhibiting qualities from two or more categories:

- ➤ The bully
- ➤ The sniper
- ➤ The victim
- ➤ The fault-finder
- ➤ The know-it-all
- ➤ The cheater

The bully

The bully is angry, abusive, abrupt, aggressive, and unpredictable. He will attempt to intimidate you into what he wants. He will explode over little things, threaten, and push you into retreating or over-reacting.

The sniper

The sniper takes potshots and makes subtle attacks. Her "humorous" put-downs, sarcastic remarks, disapproving looks, and innuendos are a form of psychological battering.

The victim

The victim is a complainer who is fearful, has little faith in himself and others, and believes that the world is a hostile place. His negativity, resentfulness, and disappointment in life throw cold water on every idea and crush all glimmers of optimism.

The fault-finder

The fault-finder avoids taking responsibility and, instead, uses an accusatory and self-righteous tone, finding fault with everything and everyone. She is much more interested in placing blame than in finding solutions.

The know-it-all

The know-it-all is an expert who comes across like a bulldozer with an aura of personal authority that is condescending, imposing, and pompous. He knows what's wrong with every aspect of your life and is happy to tell you about it.

The cheater

The cheater uses deliberate deception to twist the facts to her benefit; her actions can border on or include theft.

The dos and don'ts of difficult people

Here are the strategies you can use to cope effectively with difficult people.

Do

List

First, *assess the situation.* Is this truly a difficult person or someone who is hungry, tired, afraid, or having a bad day?

Set boundaries and limitations regarding what you will and will not tolerate.

Seek understanding of their true motivation. Be willing to listen attentively, even if someone initially seems out of line. Allow the difficult person a chance to blow off steam and feel heard. (Set a time limit for this interchange.)

When it serves your ultimate intention to be on the same "team" as the difficult person, *find a common goal, intention, or "enemy"* that you share.

Make *"I want to find solutions that work for both of us"* your mantra when dealing with a difficult person. Keep reminding him that finding a mutually acceptable solution is your goal.

Insist on a problem-solving approach, with complaints and suggestions for resolution in writing.

Require the citing of specifics rather than accepting sweeping generalizations.

Respond to pot-shots and attacks with a question. "That sounds like you're making fun of me. Are you?" The response may be one of denial ("I'm only joking!"), but nevertheless, questioning these attacks will reduce them in the future.

Take an unpredictable action to get their attention: drop a book, stand up, or firmly call them by name.

Use the broken record technique. When the difficult person insists on debating an issue you believe is already decided, calmly keep repeating the same response.

Stop and move on. Difficult people often have an insatiable appetite for more. When you believe you have done enough to appease, move on.

Give them the last word, because that gives you the last action.

Sometimes, we have to *cut our losses.* It may be worth the loss to cut the difficult person out of your life, if possible.

Don't

List

Don't debate their negative outlook. Instead, respond with your own optimistic expectations.

Don't try to beat a difficult person at their own game. There is often no point fighting back or using reason. They have been practicing their skills for a lifetime, and you're an amateur. Express your views only when you can avoid the battle for right and wrong.

Don't become emotionally involved and caught up in the cycle. Try to take a detached, impersonal view.

Don't try to change the difficult person. You can only change your responses to their behavior.

Don't interpret their behavior as a personal attack. The difficult person's bad behavior is not about you.

Remember

Dealing with difficult people takes practice, so don't give up or get discouraged. Although these strategies won't change the difficult person, they will challenge their ability to interfere in your life.

Summary

You are now prepared to use conversation to clear the air and create a sense of connection and dedication to starting over with a clean slate. In this chapter, you learned the following:

- ➤ How to hold a difficult discussion
- ➤ How to analyze and define an issue that is fueling a workplace conflict
- ➤ How to fight smart and fight fair
- ➤ How to make a magical apology
- ➤ How to deal with difficult people

In our next and final chapter, you will see exactly how you can build on what you've learned throughout this book to make real positive changes in your workplace (and your life).

>7

Making Conflict Management Happen in Your Workplace

Women face unique challenges in the workplace. Women in management and leadership positions have additional hurdles to overcome. One day, women will be valued and rewarded for their relational abilities. However, that day is not here yet, so it's critical that you continue to hone your skills and find the balance that works for you. Reading this book is an important step in becoming a gifted manager and leader.

It's easy to ignore conflicts between employees and hope that they will disappear or resolve themselves. However, that is a terrible management strategy. At this point in time, you have the knowledge necessary to deal with the conflicts that typically erupt in the workplace. This section will give you what you need to use those skills when you are in a leadership position. In this chapter you will learn the following:

> ➤ Techniques to foster employee loyalty
> ➤ How to design a conflict-management system for your workplace

Employee loyalty

Your employees can make you or break you. Your best chance at having employees who will go out of their way to help you and your business succeed is if they are inspired to be loyal. Loyal employees:

> ➤ Are more likely to be productive.

> ➤ Tend to stay put, which helps keep the costs of recruiting and training new hires to a minimum. However, don't confuse longevity with loyalty. Just because someone is there long term doesn't mean that she is loyal.

> ➤ Promote satisfaction among your clients/customers, encouraging loyalty among them too. Loyal customers (also known as repeat business) are less price sensitive, and they bring in referrals for new business.

Employee-loyalty blueprint

Here is what you need to do to inspire and foster loyalty in your company.

Set a good example

Show your employees that you take work seriously. If you are out shopping or busy making plans for the weekend, your employees will follow suit.

Create clear boundaries

Your employees can have many friends, but only one employer. Yes, you want to be friendly, but not at the cost of eroding your unique role and position. Most employees will be delighted to have a boss who can be depended upon to make difficult decisions, call the shots, and resolve awkward or burdensome problems—tasks they would never present to a friend or coworker.

Outline each employee's sphere of influence

Each staff member should be clear about where their own domain starts and stops. This kind of definition fosters a sense of pride while preventing boundary overstepping and turf wars between employees.

Show your employees that you are loyal to them

Never belittle or criticize an employee in public. Avoid threats or any action that might give an employee a reason to question your commitment to them. Instead, carefully present your criticisms and see "mistakes" as opportunities for learning.

Give your employees something to be proud of

Strive to make your organization the best it can be. Whether you are the CEO of a large corporation, a supervisor in a government organization, or running a Mom-and-Pop shop, you want your product and service to shine so that everyone involved has a sense of pride and accomplishment.

Do good deeds

Have an outreach plan that gives both you and your employees a chance to interact with and give back to the larger community in a positive way.

Reward your employees

Money cannot buy loyalty, but money does serve as a metaphor, telling your employees how much you value them. Fair wages, appropriate raises, and an occasional unexpected treat can go a long way in building loyal employees.

Cultivate peak performance

Provide your employees with training and development opportunities so that they can learn and grow. As they develop, challenge them to set and meet high expectations.

Foster a team mentality

Encourage your employees to communicate their ideas and allow them to influence company practices and policies. Likewise, share your own vision for the future and your thoughts on how you will all get there together.

Recognize and respond

Everyone appreciates positive feedback. Once it becomes clear that you are willing and able to provide it, most employees will go the extra mile in order to get it.

Build solid relationships

Find common ground, share life experiences, prove your trustworthiness, and be patient, as strong relationships blossom over time.

Be yourself

Find your own management style. Somewhere between "surrogate mother" who is more of a care-giver than the boss and the stereotypical "conniving ice-queen" who responds to employees with contempt and ridicule, each of us must find our own happy medium.

Remember the platinum rule

Above all, as you go about your business, remember that each employee must be seen as an individual—what works in some cases will bring disaster in another. Forget the golden rule—don't treat your employees as you want to be treated. Instead, find out what each of them needs and wants, and treat them as they want to be treated.

Creating a conflict-management program for your workplace

One key strategy to manage workplace conflicts is having a system or program in place to handle conflicts as they arise. This section will teach you how to create that system so that you can deflect potential problems before they become destructive.

Whenever people work together, misunderstandings or disagreements will inevitably occur. In many situations, the parties involved can work out their dispute without involving others or adversely affecting workplace harmony. However, timing is critical. Allowing a conflict to run its own course can backfire when it drags out, and irreparable damage is done to a relationship or to morale. The key in many situations is to have a process in place so that remedies are readily accessible before tempers flare out of control and the situation gets out of hand.

In *Chapter 4, Conflict Management Styles, Strategies, and Methods*, you learned how seven conflict-management methods (insight, negotiation, facilitation, mediation, arbitration, litigation, and unilateral power) can each be used to manage conflict. In this section, we are going to take this knowledge a step further as I introduce you to the concept of **Conflict Management System Design**.

When personality clashes disrupt teamwork, productivity, and effectiveness, an intervention is often necessary. If a conflict-savvy supervisor is available to intervene, they may be able to bring about resolution. However, sometimes a supervisor's intervention is not enough, or the supervisor may be viewed as the actual problem. In these instances, having customized formal and informal processes in place to address workplace disputes can be critical. Conflict Management System Design refers to the proactive development, in consultation with employees, of a customized plan or program, which is the Conflict Management System or **CMS.** It includes formal and informal structures and procedures to address workplace conflict.

Alternative Dispute Resolution (ADR) and Internal Dispute Resolution (IDR)

Frequently, any conflict-management method outside of court litigation or another formal administrative proceeding is referred to as **Alternative Dispute Resolution** or **ADR**. ADR processes focus on interest, rather than rights or power to settle disputes. (Remember, in the Lemon story from *Chapter 4, Conflict Management Styles, Strategies, and Methods,* the sisters' interests were the rind, the juice, and the seeds. Once we understood each sister's interests, it didn't matter who had a legal right to the lemon.)

Interest-based ADR processes are generally considered faster and more user-friendly methods of conflict management than traditional, formal approaches. These processes (such as facilitation and mediation) empower disputing parties to jointly craft resolutions that meet their needs rather than focus on their legal or organizational rights.

Sometimes, the use of ADR processes within an organization is referred to as **Internal Dispute Resolution** (**IDR**). IDR is on the rise for a number of reasons including a growing concern for employee rights, the decline in unionization that has resulted in the unavailability of grievance procedures, and the emphasis on controlling costs.

IDR and other ADR processes can provide innovative alternatives to arbitrary office purges. However, before an organization devises a Conflict Management System that uses the ADR or IDR process, there are various factors to consider. Here is what you need to know.

Establishing goals

The goal of a well-designed CMS is to bring employee grievances to light by whatever mechanism works best and to defuse as many grievances as possible at an early stage, long before anyone is tempted to call in lawyers. Most ADR processes focus on privacy and strive to avoid the potential embarrassment and unfavorable consequences of a public trial.

Having a CMS in place means that it is legitimate to question authority. An organization's culture has to be prepared to accept this. Along these lines, conflict-management training for managers is essential. This training should not center on legal questions but on how to listen to people, understand their motivations, and assess how the manager's own actions may be perceived.

Gathering input

It is vital that input be gathered from all stakeholders before a CMS is created. This input into the design and development of the system will help ensure a sense of ownership and the perception that the program meets their needs. The necessary stakeholders include the potential complainants, respondents, and bystanders (the rest of the workforce) in the organization. This input will also help develop the new system's credibility and ensure that upper management—or outside consultants—don't design a CMS and hand it down to managers and employees for their use.

Structuring the CMS

Conflict Management Systems can be structured in a variety of ways. What is most important is that all employees understand and respect the CMS. There is no need for expensive or sophisticated options. Instead, the focus should be on making the program approachable and responsive. A CMS should be designed so that the possible outcomes include anything the parties can imagine and agree upon. This is broader than the legal solutions that a judge or jury could impose.

At their simplest, CMSs start with an open-door policy that encourages employees to bring grievances of any kind to their managers, with the assurance that no retaliation will follow. Details such as how the complaints are expressed (verbally or in writing) and how they are channeled depend on several factors, including the company's size and culture. (The open-door policy should be coupled with training for managers so that they know how to react to people when a problem exists.)

Larger organizations can create CMSs with more options. However, sometimes, interest-based processes are difficult to implement in large organizations. Corporations, by definition, are rights and power-based structures. People in rights and power-based structures typically default to rights or power-based conflict-management processes.

The CMS design process should make sense for the particular organization. Since each organization already has its own unique, prescribed policies and practices, it may be necessary to experiment and test processes before arriving at those that best meet with the organization's structure and objectives. There is no one-size-fits-all solution. It is important, however, to keep all policies and procedures as simple as possible, with a minimum of structure and bureaucracy. This can be achieved by starting with the simplest options first and moving progressively up toward the more complex ones.

Components of a CMS

Any complete system will incorporate the following:

> ➤ An investigation process
>
> ➤ An opportunity to explore options through dialogue between the parties
>
> ➤ Access to formal rights-based processes
>
> ➤ Ongoing training to teach and reinforce the program's objectives
>
> ➤ Feedback mechanisms to allow for revisions to the process as needs change

Ultimately, any process that meets the parties' needs may be used in your CMS. For example, staff members at the **Los Alamos National Laboratory** (**LANL**) use a process that they call "dual-advocacy mediation." This method requires that each of the parties in conflict have a mediator who also acts as a personal advocate. Here are some suggestions of components that can be included in your organization's CMS:

Hotline

This is a confidential service staffed by company "advisors." The advisor should be a volunteers trained in conflict management, effective listening, ethics, and confidentiality. These advisors can answer questions, act as go-betweens, review options, get the facts, help open doors, or refer to other resources.

Open-door policy

Employees are encouraged to meet with their immediate supervisor or any other manager to discuss problems. Employees may or may not be required to seek resolution at the lowest level before approaching the next level of management, including the organization's most senior executives. For the open-door policy to work, there must be a clear and enforced prohibition of retaliation against the system's users.

Senior-management review

This variation on the open-door policy gives employees an opportunity to discuss unresolved problems or complaints with a board or committee of management personnel, the president, or CEO.

Peer review

Unresolved issues go to a review committee or board made up of other employees.

Ombudsperson

An individual is designated to investigate and provide advice and assistance to employees with concerns or complaints, act as a liaison between management and employees or coworkers, and help resolve various disputes, including customer disputes. Usually, the ombudsperson is from an independent office.

Grievance procedure

A grievance procedure is a formal multistep process that outlines the procedures to bring a complaint to progressively higher levels of authority.

Conciliation

Conciliation is an informal process by which a passive third party is positioned between disputing parties in order to create a channel for communication. This is generally done by conveying messages between parties who are unwilling to meet face-to-face. Often, the hope is to identify common interests and to eventually re-establish direct communication.

Mediation

Mediation is an informal and confidential process whereby an impartial third party with no decision-making power facilitates discussions between disputing parties to help them bring a resolution to the issues at hand. The mediator establishes ground rules for negotiation, opens up the channels of communication, identifies the issues, helps the parties explore options for settlement, and occasionally makes recommendations on the issues in dispute. In mediation, it is the parties that make the final decision as to a resolution of their issues.

Arbitration

Arbitration is a formal process in which a third party listens to the parties' presentation of evidence and arguments and then makes a decision as to what the outcome should be. The decision may or may not be binding.

Management changes

When other interventions seem unable to effectively handle workplace conflict, the solution may require a change in management or management style. A management team may need to step in, evaluate, and take appropriate steps to rectify the management's behavior or style. Department reorganizing, a change in company policy, monetary compensation, or an apology from the management may be what is called for.

Appeals

An appeal component should be incorporated into your CMS plans to address one or both parties' dissatisfaction with the conflict's outcome or resolution. While there is no one right answer, whatever the appeals process is, it must be set in place and available to all system users.

Make a note

All CMSs should include written policies that are examined by an attorney.

Day-to-day action points

While adopting a formal conflict-management program will work wonders, it is important to remember the smaller day-to-day actions that you can take to deal with conflict in your workplace. Some of the following strategies will work best when you are a party to the conflict, and others are most effective when you are stepping into a conflict that others are involved in:

> ➤ Think back to what you've learned throughout this book and consider how you might use this information to safely bring conflict out into the open, de-escalate negative confrontations, and stop potentially devastating conflicts in their tracts.

> ➤ Confront others privately to prevent embarrassment.

➤ Seek a balance between intervening too quickly and encouraging or leaving workers to settle conflicts on their own.

➤ Clearly define lines of authority to eliminate "turf wars" or power struggles.

➤ Impose a "gag order" or "cooling-off period."

➤ Ask everyone involved to write down their side of the dispute and their recommended remedies.

➤ Use counseling and other community resources to provide services to those who are struggling with ongoing conflict issues.

➤ Deal with office politics by avoiding the rumor mill.

➤ Gain insight into the work style and habits of supervisors and coworkers.

➤ Keep your cool—uncontrolled emotions can harm your image, no matter how much you are provoked.

➤ If stories are inconsistent or the cause of the conflict is undeterminable, at an appropriate time, suggest wiping the slate clean and starting anew, by putting the incident in the past.

➤ When an argument escalates so that people are no longer listening to each other, call a time-out. Sometimes, all that's necessary is a few minutes, but a few hours or days may be the best prescription.

➤ Schedule a staff meeting or an all-day retreat to deal specifically with conflict management.

➤ Saying "How can I help you?' rather than "What do you want?" may be all it takes to stop a conflict from escalating. Realize that the way something is said is probably more important than what is said (it's all in the delivery).

➤ Encourage a team approach to problem solving (in some companies, a team approach may require a complete culture change).

➤ Conduct fair investigations. This will help build trust and create an atmosphere conducive to collaborative dispute resolution.

➤ Make a preliminary diagnosis as to the causes of the conflict and discuss it with the disputants to get their input. Their input will be necessary for making a definitive diagnosis.

➤ Don't force apologies.

➤ Bully tactics backfire. Avoid them at all costs. This includes asking someone to compromise just to be a good sport. Unwilling agreements often carry resentments that cause more trouble later on.

➤ When looking at the effects of a conflict incident, consider the effects on both parties, others, and the organization.

➤ Model good practice. Management should be available, approachable and visible. Your positive and negative attitudes are contagious.

➤ Identify the source of conflict and evaluate if the conflict is structural—arising from company policies and procedures—or interpersonal.

Summary

In this chapter, you learned:

- ➤ Techniques to foster employee loyalty
- ➤ How to design a conflict-management system for your workplace
- ➤ The little (but important) things to remember when dealing with day-to-day conflict

This brings us on to...

The bottom line

You are now a conflict-management expert. WOW!! But, guess what? You are still human. So, while you are capable of intervening and helping manage conflicts at work, you may still fall prey to your own conflicts when your reptilian brain is pushed into high gear. So, it is critical that you share this book with your co-workers. If enough people in your workplace are wise in the ways of conflict management, you will each be able to step in and help each other before a conflict becomes destructive.

In my own life, there have been instances where someone was willing to walk into one of my conflicts and act as the mediator. I am so grateful for these people. Other times, no one came forward, and the results were disastrous.

Please do not hesitate to e-mail me with your feedback and questions.

All the best,

Elinor.